Point of
VIEW and the
EMOTIONAL
Arc of Stories

A handbook for writers and storytellers

"Brilliant and original! This is a must-have handbook, full of useful insights and practical instructions. A great gift from two of the best teachers I've known."

—Noa Baum, storyteller and author

Point of VIEW and the EMOTIONAL Arc of Stories

A handbook for writers and storytellers

LOREN NIEMI & NANCY DONOVAL

Parkhurst Brothers Publishers

MARION, MICHIGAN

www.parkhurstbrothers.com

Consumers may order Parkhurst Brothers books from their favorite online or bricks-and-mortar booksellers, expecting prompt delivery. Parkhurst Brothers books are distributed to the trade through the Chicago Distribution Center. Trade and library orders may be placed through Ingram Book Company, Baker & Taylor, Follett Library Resources and other book industry wholesalers. To order from Chicago Distribution Center, phone 800-621-2736 or fax to 800-621-8476. Copies of this and other Parkhurst Brothers Publishers titles are available to organizations and corporations for purchase in quantity by contacting Special Sales Department at our home office location, listed on our website. Manuscript submission guidelines for this publishing company are available at our website.

Printed in the United States of America
First Edition, July 2020
Printing history: 2020 2021 2022   8 7 6 5 4 3 2 1

ISBN: Trade Paperback   978-1-62491-161-3
ISBN: e-book   978-1-62491-162-0

Parkhurst Brothers Publishers believes that the free and open exchange of ideas is essential for the maintenance of our freedoms. We support the First Amendment of the United States Constitution and encourage citizens to study all sides of public policy questions, making up their own minds.

Cover design by: Linda D. Parkhurst
Interior design by: Susan Harring
Proofreading by: Bill and Barbara Paddack
Acquired for Parkhurst Brothers Publishers
And edited by: Ted Parkhurst
Data management by: Linda D. Parkhurst

072020

Loren's Dedication

For LouAnn who asked the question

and

Debra who sat with me while I wrote the answer

Nancy's Dedication

For my

Dad

who gave me my sense of humor,

a sense of play, and a love of words, and for my

Mom

who showed me how to treasure people

above everything.

Loren's Acknowledgements

I acknowledge each of these exquisite exemplars
of what this book explores:
Clare Murphy and Mora Menzes
who embody the world of traditional stories;
Ward Rubrecht and Raymond Christian
who embody the rich possibilities of the "slam" form;
Brother Blue and Minton Sparks
who embody the poetic point of view;
Bil Lepp and Regi Carpenter
who embody humor as critique; and
Laura Packer and Elizabeth Ellis
who embody the nuance of craft.

Nancy's Acknowledgements

I am profoundly grateful to all my mentors, friends, and colleagues for nurturing, sustaining and stretching me into the storyteller, teacher, and story coach I've become: Rives Collins recruited me into storytelling and teaching; Janice Del Negro hired me for my first paid gig; Jim May and Dan Keding booked me for my first festivals; Syd Lieberman modeled excellence down to the bone; Beth Horner and Susan O'Halloran, sisters-in-arms for art-making and life-living; Gerald Fierst and David Novak, boundary pushing co-conspirators; the whole Wild Onion Storytelling Festival extended family; my beloved peer coaching Porcupines; my home communities in Chicago, Minneapolis/St. Paul and now Tennessee; and every storytelling student and coaching client for trusting and teaching me. Each name stands for fifty more. And, of course, Loren Niemi, my teaching/consulting partner extraordinaire.

Contents

Introduction

This book is a meditation on two fundamental aspects of story-making: point of view and the emotional arc of a story. Throughout, I am going to press a fundamental question: what is the result of the choices you make to bring a story to life? Also throughout, I will use variations of *Little Red Riding Hood* as examples of the various points I am trying to make.

While it is helpful if you have read *The New Book of Plots* before or soon after this text, each book is a distinct but complementary exploration of core questions for narrative creation. This book is not intended as an extension of *The New Book of Plots* as you do not need to have read it to find this useful, but it is my bias as the author of both that when paired they will give you a substantial set of tools for crafting engaging stories whether written or oral, personal or traditional in form.

I've always thought of *The New Book of Plots* as a meditation on narrative progression with sample stories accompanied by how-to exercises that illustrate ten kinds of useful narrative (plot) forms. They are:

- **Straight (Traditional) Narratives** begin at the beginning and proceed to an end.

- **Digression**, in which the bulk of the story is in the form of humorous or serious detours.
- **Revelation**, in which something is withheld which answers the central question of the story.
- **Reversal** (also know as Mirror Plots), where the audience is asked to rethink what is what and who is who.
- **Flashbacks** begin at a moment, go back in time and return to that moment again.
- **A String of Pearls** is a series of vignettes around a central, often unstated, theme.
- **A List Story** is literally a list (or a formulaic grouping) of vignettes organized by number or a category.
- **Regression**, beginning at the chronological end and moving backward to the beginning.
- **Parallel Plots**, where two related stories are told simultaneously.
- **Meta-narration**, in which the author/narrator comments on the story as they tell it.

These plot types can be arranged as "points on a compass," serving as a guide on the path to the development of the story. The four cardinal points (N-S-E-W) represent the most commonly used plot forms (straight narrative, revelation, flashback and parallel plot) and the other points (NE-SE-SW-NW) represent mixed forms or interesting variations (digression, mirror, regression and meta-narrated) which serve particular kinds of narrative purposes.

If we begin with the realization that there are many ways to tell a story, the choice of one plot form or another rests with how you want the audience to experience the story. Does the story require a straightforward progression or is there a value in taking liberties with the sequence – going backwards or telling two stories at once? Do you trust the audience or yourself to take the "road less traveled"? Once you know the permissions and limitations of the plot forms, you can test whether one path or another will best serve to move the audience into and through the landscape of the story.

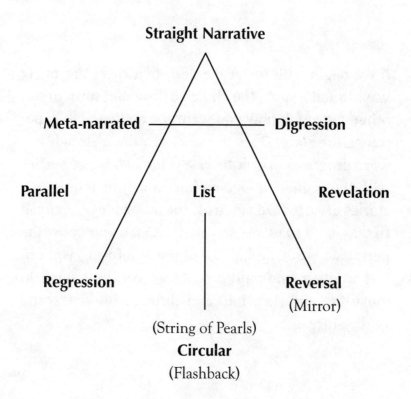

If *The New Book of Plots* is about structuring the sequence of events or developments in a story, this book is about the necessary creation of the characters, colors and textures that make those narratives come alive, the "how" you illustrate that landscape. The decision to suspend our habitual grasp upon the here-and-now and agree to dwell "In the Land of ..." story rests on many specific decisions, but two – the emotional arc of the story and the "voice" of the narrator – are interconnected and the focus of this book.

The **Action** (what happens) does not exist in a vacuum but in a time and place that the audience – whether reading or hearing – must "see" in their imagination. The simple fact is that the audience has a series of responses (*liking* the story *or not* being the most obvious) to the material based on the way the narrative is fleshed out. It is the function of that fleshing out, the choices you make of point of view, present or past tense, the description of character and culture that offer (or in some cases withhold) what the audience will use to augment their own imaginative engagement with the material.

Who Will Find This Book Helpful?

In the years since the publication of *The New Book of Plots*, several teachers of composition and fiction have told me that what their students need is *not* help with plot forms. I'm told that they have too many and too clichéd plots available to them. Instead, I've been told that what young writers need is guidance in developing characters and help to shape the milieu those characters inhabit – the world in which those plots take place. This book is my offer of assistance in doing just that.

This book is for authors, storytellers and would-be storytellers whether you call yourself a storyteller, writer, spoken word performer or something else. Whatever the name, the benefit you derive from the application of this material to your creative process will come from a better understanding of how narrative content is shaped. The material in this book has been developed in workshops with storytellers and writers since 1986. In the course of those thirty-some years, I have seen students discover their authentic voices by experimenting with new approaches to telling and writing stories. Good for them for exploring new strategies. In the process of teaching it, this material has helped me refine my thinking and improve my own storytelling.

Because I am first and foremost a storyteller working mostly in the oral tradition, much of what I say is framed around the creation of stories as oral performance pieces. However, the concepts and exercises recommended here will apply to written material as well. Whether your delivery is oral or written, this book is about the choices we make to craft an emotional arc and create appropriate points of view to support the story; and how those choices help or hinder the transmission of the narrative's meaning of the story to an audience.

If, as Elizabeth Ellis says, "the function of a narrator is to be **the reliable guide** taking us into dangerous lands and safely back again," it will fall to the narrative voice to facilitate that journey. Does the audience trust the narrator? Like them? Want to go further? The narrative voice, whether speaking in the first, second or third person, in the present or in the past tense, provides a framework for how the audience understands the characters in the story and the story itself. Those specific choices we make about what is told and how it is told also create the emotional arc – the feeling of engagement – with the story.

It is the construction of point of view and the emotional arc that suggests how the audience should feel about the world of the story and in many stories to prompt their own memories of similar times, places or situations. How we tell a story can make all the difference between an audience seeing themselves as sharing the hero or heroine's experience or standing at a distance questioning the machinations of the narrative unfold.

A Note About the Examples Used in This Text

My task in writing this is to help you identify the specific choices within the narrative - to illuminate the do's and don'ts, the permissions and limitations - for crafting both that narrative voice and the emotional arc of the story. In some chapters, I will offer specific exercises you can do to help in your story creation.

Since I believe that there is a value in demonstrating that of which I speak, I will offer examples of *Little Red Riding Hood* and some personal stories at particular points along the way.

It is appropriate at this junction to say that I am using three historical versions of *Little Red Riding Hood*. In the first and oldest, the wolf eats the girl - end of story. In the second, the wolf is a metaphor, and rather than eat her he "deflowers" her. It is the third version, the one associated with the Brothers Grimm, in which she is eaten and then saved by the intervention of the Hunter (or Woodsman) that you probably are most familiar with. To keep it interesting, I will use any of those versions for the examples.

Are you ready? If so, let us begin.

Section One
In the Land of ...

Chapter One
The Importance of Inviting an Audience into the World

It is often said that you should begin at the beginning. But which is the right beginning?

"Once upon a time ..." is the way many folk and fairy tales in the European tradition begin. It is an invitation to enter another time and place, to suspend our judgment of the possible and how the world works. The fact is that while that phrase is a shorthand invitation, folk and fairy tales are not complete worlds in themselves but rather blueprints for worlds. That *"Once upon a time ..."* is a starting point with a time (usually indistinct), a place (often unnamed but generic: a forest or a castle or some such) and characters (a boy, a girl, a king, a witch) as suggestions attached to the frame of a plot. All of it is subject to expansion. In

traditional practice, the teller would add details to flesh out the story in ways that were relevant to the audience.

This still happens today. Look at the raft of television and movie adaptations of familiar stories – *Snow White*, *Beauty and the Beast*, *Cinderella* – in which the bare frame of the narrative that has come down over the centuries has been expanded to meet the conventions of contemporary media forms. What is your pleasure? Picture book? Big effects movie? Animated cartoon? Broadway musical? Role-playing game?

This is also true of personal stories, though we usually do not think we are using a formulaic beginning. What we do have is an anecdotal core of the story that we expand and enrich in relation to our audiences. The same narrative core can be a five-minute slam story, ten minutes of amusement for co-workers, or family lore told and retold at every wedding, funeral or holiday gathering. Once we know what kind of a story we need it to be, we often select a formulaic beginning: *"I remember the time ..."* *"Did I ever tell you about ..."* or *"You're not going to believe this, but ..."*

The value of the formulaic opening in any culture is that it asks us to set aside one kind of assumption in favor of another. The everyday world of cause and effect, of roles and expectations, can be upended. Will be. The logic of the everyday world is surrendered to another kind of thought, one in which magic exists in all its forms. Once we offer the formula beginning, whether *"Once upon a time"* or *"Crick Crack"* or a more contemporary *"In a galaxy far, far away ..."* the listener or reader is swept into a story that is not bound by everyday experience and expectation.

That formulaic beginning does not, however, relieve us of the task of creating a compelling image to begin with. We need to bring the audience into the world of which we speak.

> Once upon a time, there was a little girl, cute as a button and well-loved by her mother and grandmother. So well-loved that she was spoiled. So loved and so spoiled that her grandmother made her a red cloak and matching cap that the girl wore whenever she went out.

Well, there's a beginning. That is pretty much the traditional Brothers Grimm beginning of *Little Red Riding Hood*. It tells us something about the heroine of the story and promises us more detail as we go along. It is a starting point but frankly not a terribly exciting one, and it is certainly not the only possible starting point.

Here's another:

No one had been to visit for days. Did they not know that she was old and frail or that her cataracts had brought her into a perpetual gloom of shadows, so that she dare not venture out of her house? Did her daughter not care? Could she not at least send that grandchild she so loved to spend a few minutes with her if she was unwilling to come herself?

It is the same story but the focus has shifted from the girl to the grandmother and this beginning suggests it is the grandmother's story that will be told. How often do we get Grandma's point of view? As my intent in telling a story is to bring the audience into a world, why not plunge us into a less familiar but equally appropriate one?

That bringing of the audience into the world can be accomplished with a description of person, place or time. It can be done as an example by using Joseph Campbell's *The Hero's Journey* as a model, with a specific invitation to adventure or the moment the world is turned upside down.

Here that model is in brief:

I. **The Invitation**
   The hero or heroine is called to leave home/comfort
   - Willing or not
   - Knowing the task or not

2. **The Exchange**

    They meet someone who will provide assistance

    - Often their opposite – an old man, old woman or animal.
    - They prove their worth by doing what is asked of them – cut wood, carry water, release someone caught from a trap, share their food.
    - They receive directions, advice, a promise of help or a magic object, etc., that will enable them to meet the coming challenges.

3. **The Adventure**

    They face a number of challenges

    - Specific in number: 3 in Western tradition but not necessarily 3 in African, Asian or Indigenous traditions.
    - Often this is manifest as movement from external to internal – from appearances or skills to knowledge to character.
    - There may be a direct correlation between what must be learned and what is done for success.

4. **The Triumph**

    They succeed

    - The goal is obtained – the giant defeated, the treasure found, the prince or princess wooed or won.

- Internal resources, courage or wisdom are necessary for success as well as the external objects or actions.

5. **The Return**

They return to where they started
- They are recognized as the hero.
- Or not. Which often is the beginning of another story or a sequel.

Campbell is not the only model, but his is a familiar one. It starts us off quickly and moves us along a narrative line that allows for expansion as needed. It is found in many traditional stories, in contemporary media such as *Star Wars* or *Harry Potter* and can be applied to the development of our personal stories as well.

A strong beginning sets our expectations for all that follows. In traditional stories, the invitation to adventure and what is at stake is often very clear. It can be as simple as *take this basket to your Grandmother* or Helen running off with Paris and her husband calling on Odysseus to join the siege of Troy to win her back. That one is the start of two great stories – *The Iliad*, in which Odysseus is a secondary character but the man who makes the tragic end of the Trojan war possible and *The Odyssey* in which his striving to return home is the entire story. As we will see in greater detail in the following chapters, one of the functions of a strong beginning is to establish the point of view and in the best of narratives, the emotional arc of the story from the first few words.

Here are some other examples of ways to start that same story of *Little Red Riding Hood* in very different worlds.

> The oaks were old, and so close together the shadows stitched the forest into a quilt of dark and darker. Where there was light, it was a thin shaft trickling between leaves barely illuminating the stony path. When you stepped into it, you were blind, blinking to catch sight of the next step. It was an excellent place to hunt. On this morning, something red was flickering at a distance. Yes, and it was coming closer with each step through the dark to bright to dark again.

Or maybe this

> Your grandmother is ill. I want you to take her some nourishing soup and bread.

> She smells bad. I don't want to go.

> You'll smell just as bad when you're her age. Get used to it. We all do. We start decaying from inside, especially when we don't eat well or drink enough red wine.

But Mother …

Hold your tongue, child and if you have to, hold your nose when you get to her house. Here, take the basket and stay on the path. Is going and coming back easy enough a task for you? I do not want you sitting around reading foolish stories of courts and princes. That is not our life or your future. You'll not meet any prince today.

Which one would you want more of? They both take us into the same fundamental narrative but how or what that world is plays out quite differently with each choice.

Begin we must and in the telling of any story whether a familiar folk or fairy tale, a ghost story or a personal story rising from our lived experience and culture, three sets of interlocking decisions will create the world of the story:

- The first is what is the narrative progression? What happens? Literally, where do we begin and end? How do we get from that beginning to that end? This is where the decision about the plot form is made. We are not bound to a single progression and we may want to change our mind about what is the right form in relation to how we answer the following questions.

- The second is who is telling the story? Am I the

narrator discovering the story in the present tense or recounting it as something in the past? Is it being told by some third party who knows more than any of the individual characters in the story? Is the narrator impartial or do they have a stake in the story by virtue of their participation?

• The third question is what emotions or feelings are attached to the story? Another way of thinking about that is why does the story matter? How do we share what "matters" with whomever is reading or hearing the narrative? How directly or indirectly do we offer or want to invoke those feelings?

Each choice informs the others. Each choice makes the creation of the whole easier or more problematic. Ideally, we want them all to seem natural, the right words said in the right way to create a complete narrative experience.

Chapter Two
The Three Emotional Arcs of a Story

Often when I hear a discussion of the arc of the story, what is being scrutinized is actually the shape and flow of the plot itself, how one situation evolves into another with heightened tension until the writer or teller arrives at a climax. That is indeed an arc, but if we examine it closely it is not really the emotional arc, for an emotion requires a person. Plots don't feel – characters do, narrators do, the listener or reader does. And the emotional arc that any one of these feels is different than the rise and fall of action of the story itself.

Over 26 years of teaching Storytelling in the Communications and Theater programs at Metropolitan State University, and especially in the last decade when I've co-taught with Nancy Donoval, we've developed an understanding that the emotional arc is rooted in three separate and distinct arcs:

- The characters in the story.
- The narrator of the story.
- The audience reading or listening to the story.

How do they differ?

The **arc of the character** in the story is about how the characters feel about their choices or circumstances. It makes no difference whether it is a folktale or a contemporary personal story. Those who are in the story are confronted again and again with choices of what to do that can be expressed in emotional responses as well as physical acts. How do you feel standing at the side of Grandma's bed? What dominates your emotions – fear, confusion or excitement? How do you feel when your partner says they want to marry you or get a divorce? What dominates – fear, confusion or excitement? They are different stories, with the same possible responses.

If a story is about what changes from one point in a character's world to another, it is appropriate to acknowledge that not all changes are external and that the internal – the thoughts and feelings of a character – may be as much or more important to understanding how and why their world changed than what they did. While this is often central to contemporary literature (written stories) it can also be the focus of oral narratives, whether contemporary or traditional.

Here is an example of a character's emotions once again using *Little Red Riding Hood*:

> I had seen him before. Glimpsed on the street and in the park I had wondered who he was. The sleek coat, the sure swift movement, showed me that he knew his way around. I wondered what he would be like if I was close enough to touch him. I did not expect to see him here on the forest path and felt a blush creep across my face as he came closer. What would he say if he saw that scarlet which was as thrilling as it was shameful to know? What would I say? If he would think I am a naive girl, he would be right. But though I have had little experience with his kind, the curiosity was there and I knew that at some point it would burst forth.

The **arc of the narrator** has a different path, one rooted in judgment about how they – as the teller of the tale – feel about the characters in the story itself. This is the case even when the story is being told by one of the characters in the story. It may be conscious or intuitive, but a judgment of what matters, what to convey, goes to the very heart of why they are telling the story. Whether in the first or third person, the present or past tense, the narrator is making choices about how to present the story, about what needs to be said and when, what to withhold from the audience, and when. The narrator's choices determine what the audience has to work with to make the story their own.

Often it is clear that the narrator telling the story is distinct from one of the characters in the story. Sometimes it is not.

This is an old story but age is not a barrier to need. You need to hear it. I need to tell it. As is the case since Adam and Eve, this is the story of someone who is faced with a temptation and a decision. In this story, there is a girl of indistinct age. Maybe she's 10 years old, maybe older but old enough to have her mother send her by herself from one cottage to another. Still, she's young enough – or maybe foolish or distracted enough – to require a warning to stay on the path. So there's the first temptation, plain and simple. Do you listen to your mother? Do you take the instruction to heart as good advice meant to serve you well? Or do you do what the inattentive or rebellious do, stray as soon as you are out of sight?

Sometimes the relationship of the primary voice to the story is unclear. Especially at first, it may not be apparent whether the narrator is:

- the hero ... or the villain,
- a secondary character, or
- a voice outside the story itself?

Is the narrator framing the story with the intent to evoke or arrive at a particular emotion? What is the narrator's attitude about the characters and the action? Are they proud or disdainful? Are they humble? Is the narrator telling a joke, offering us an entertainment or seeking to touch our hearts with a sweet or sentimental tale? Are they providing a cautionary tale of what not to do or what lesson is to be learned from bad choices or mistaken acts?

The difference between the narrator of the story and the characters in the story may be most ambiguous in telling a personal story about your own life. How does the person who is telling that story now feel about the character **that was you** in the story? When it is your story, do you tell it as a joke at your own expense? Or with compassion for the self that has yet to learn a lesson? Is there **sympathy** or **contempt** for yourself in your narration? Does the way you tell about your feelings, choices, actions (or that of any character in the story, for that matter) change as the narrative proceeds?

When you are writing or telling a story *from your own experience*, it is important to remember that the historical character representing you is always discussed in the past tense. He or she played a part in your becoming who you are as narrator, but time has passed ... And in that time, you have adopted an attitude about the "you" who plays a part in the story.

Those same questions of the narrator's judgment in personal stories can apply to traditional material. Here is our core story again:

> I'll admit that I learned a lesson. Perhaps not the one you assume would come from bedding him. I was going to spill that blood sooner or later. Oh, I would have liked it to have been a prince or a man who could be my church-blessed husband but times being what they are, it was just as likely that I would be taken by robbers or drunken soldiers or my own kin. Why not have my maidenhood taken by one who had no thought of anything but the ravenous pleasure of now? I did not enjoy it. You can hardly expect me to have but what I did enjoy was the ease with which I made my escape. Seeing him in his stupor, thinking that if he tied a cord around my ankle that it would be enough to keep me there. Foolish, yes – the both of us. Me for entering the room and him for letting me leave it.

In a well-crafted story, we'd like to have the audience understand who the narrator is fairly soon. This may be determined in part by the choice of the first or third person, and by the use of present or past tense. Who the narrator is and why they are telling us this story will also be determined by the author/teller's having the narrator approve or disapprove of the choices, responses and relationships of the characters in the story as they present it. Those choices determine the focus and whether the meaning of the story is explicit or obscure.

Finally, there is the **arc of the audience**. What or how does the audience feel about the characters in the story? How did you feel about that last example? Are you satisfied, disturbed, uneasy but willing to suspend judgment? Where does the audience lean in sympathetically or shrink back in fright? What are the specific elements that engage them from beginning to end? How do you as the creator of a narrative encourage them to feel particular emotions as you go?

Though I'll go into detail about the mechanics of **the audience's emotional arc** later, I will say that of the three kinds of emotional arc, this is the one the writer or storyteller has the least control over. Yet, in the end, it is the one that matters – the one in which the audience or reader takes the story to heart as their own.

The three emotional arcs of a story can be correlated to the relationship that is at the center of the very act of crafting or presenting the material. It is the essential *ménage a trois* of the story itself with the teller presenting and the audience receiving. Each is independent – the story, the teller and the audience – with separate and distinct characteristics in relationship to the other two.

The teller has a relationship to the story and the audience. His or her responsibility is to know the story, to like it enough to craft it and then to "transfer" it to the audience orally or in written form. Knowing the story includes understanding the emotional arc of the characters in the story. As a teller you have to know more than you say, the "what" and "why" of the story, even if you do not actually tell everything you know. The transfer of the story may be seen as corresponding to the emotional arc of the narrator. How you tell the story says as much about your commitment to it as whatever happens in the story itself. The audience looks to you for clues as to how they should feel.

The audience has a relationship grounded in trust and permission with the teller and the story. They have to trust the teller and then come to the story through the narrator's arc. Before the audience can embrace the material, they have to first be receptive to the story's presentation, in effect giving permission to the teller to offer the gift. While I am tempted to go into some detail about the importance of how the storyteller presents themselves before they say the first word, this will take us on a detour. Let's simply say, an audience's judgment of whether you can be "trusted" begins as soon as you set foot on the stage.

We deem narrators who we do not trust as unreliable. This can be a conscious decision on the part of the teller but let's not go into detail about that now. For now, let's posit that the norm is for the teller to be trustworthy.

As much as the narrator's arc is designed to give the audience clues about how to feel, the audience enters the story through their own arc. The story makes sense or it doesn't. It has emotional resonance or it doesn't. It entertains or it doesn't. It means something to them in the moment (and hopefully after the fact) or it doesn't. The teller can never be sure of those responses, but if the teller is doing their job, it is easier for the audience to come to a relationship with the story that approximates the teller's intent. Ultimately if the audience has a relationship to the story, it will stick, i.e., be remembered and have meaning. If they don't it will be as ephemeral as a wisp of smoke.

Let's look at each of them in greater detail.

The Arc of the Character in the Story

Whether it is a traditional folk/fairy tale or your personal story, things happen and the characters in the story have feelings about what is happening. In folktales, the emotional arc of the character is not always stated. That is mostly a function of the folktale as a narrative blueprint, rather than as a fully fleshed out performance. As it is told to a specific audience in a specific cultural setting, the narrator can fill in the appropriate emotional detail for any of the characters in the story as they are telling it.

We are not told how Little Red Riding Hood feels about meeting the wolf. Curious? Frightened? A bit guilty that she has not followed her mother's instructions and (at his suggestion) strayed off the path? All of them are possible. Depending on the storyteller and audience, you might want to articulate any one of them. The emotional arc of the character is their response to the rise and fall, the twists and turns of the narrative progression. Articulating it, or some portion of it, allows for greater complexity and texture for the story as a whole when we acknowledge their internal thoughts, their feelings about the choices and actions unfolding in the story.

Why?

The value in giving voice to the inner life of a character is making them "real" for the audience by providing more for the reader or listener to connect to. We don't have to articulate the emotional arc of every character but the fact is that any character in *Little Red Riding Hood,* including Grandma and the wolf, will have feelings about the setting in which they find themselves and their choices, their actions or those of the other characters. How does the wolf feel about Red Riding Hood or Grandma? Is this devouring a matter of necessity or of choice? Is he (or she) more than the cliché of "... the better to eat you, my dear"?

To that parenthesis: why should we assume that the wolf is male? What difference would having a female wolf make to the wolf's actions in the traditional story? How does the dynamic of her "hunger" change when the gender shifts? What emotional responses would switching to a "she-wolf" offer to our understanding of the character or role of predator and prey?

> The smell of the basket was powerful. There was sausage and something baked. Bread or a cake perhaps. The pups would enjoy something exotic after weeks of rabbit and squirrel. But as powerful a temptation as the scent was, the other scent – that of a menstruating woman – was more than she could bear. Attracted to the blood call, she was wary ... For where there is a female ready for mating there is often a male armed with an axe or gun. She would have to observe this one to see if she would be worth the effort.

In the oldest versions of *Little Red Riding Hood*, the wolf eats her, end of story. It may be factual but not necessarily a satisfying ending for the audience (though it may be quite satisfying for the wolf). Whether male or female, in that version it makes no difference. It is the wolf's essential hunger that drives the action and Little Red Riding Hood is served up as a reminder that misfortune comes to us all.

In the next variation of the story, the "wolf" has "his" way with her. Here the assignment of specific gender extends the idea of a wolf from a four-legged predator to a sexual metaphor. In that version, our heroine is not "devoured" in a literal sense. Rather, she is assaulted – the direct result of speaking to the wolf and then straying from the path. And having strayed, the violation is compensation for her error. Thereafter, only her own cunning saves her from further harm. After being deflowered, she declares that she has to go relieve (or in some variants, clean) herself. The wolf grants her permission to do so provided he ties a rope to her leg. Once she is safely out of sight she unties it from her ankle, reties it to a chair (or tree) and departs for home "wiser for the experience" as one variant puts it.

This version of the wolf as metaphor carries a double-edged message. On the one hand, it is clearly a **cautionary metaphor** that men will prey upon girls. On the other, it offers a **lesson** that girls cannot depend on anyone to save them but themselves. The second lesson does not negate the first but it does provide a more satisfying ending than the version of the story in which she's dinner.

It is in the Brothers Grimm version that we step back from the sexual metaphor to soften the hard moral of the story with the introduction of two things that have gotten stuck in our cultural landscape.

The first is the introduction of that repetitious variation of call and response:

"What big ears you have!"
" The better to hear you."
"What big eyes you have!"
"The better to see you."
"What big hands you have!"
"The better to hold you."
"Oh, what a big mouth you have!"

Oh, how many storytellers have milked those phrases for effect!

The second is the introduction of the hunter – or as he is called in some versions, the woodsman – as a kind of *Deus Ex Machina* to swoop in and save our heroine. Oh, and Grandma, too, by cutting the wolf's belly open with a knife (or scissors) at which point both Grandma and the kid emerge whole and, if we are to believe the Grimms' text, none the worse for being swallowed.

Don't bother with the failure of logic and biology that they would be swallowed whole and return unharmed or that a sleeping wolf would not wake up when you slit his (or her) belly. By this point in the tale, we have abandoned everything but the notion that we need a "happy" ending.

In every version of this story, the core narrative is one of going to Grandma's, meeting a wolf who proceeds to Grandma's before our heroine, disposing of Grandma and then the child confronted by the wolf, and leading to a resolution of the story. It is a straightforward narrative progression. The endings are very different over time – gobbled up, untying a rope to slip away, being swallowed whole and saved by a huntsman – but in every version the substance of the story is spare enough to invite descriptive detailing of the component actions to suit the age and circumstances of the audience. The plot, such as it is, begs for elaboration and details, including the emotional responses of one or more characters to the action.

I will again note that throughout this book I have and will continue to use each of those three variants in my examples. Whether the first, second or more familiar Brothers

Grimm version, the story I am telling is *Little Red Riding Hood* from as many points of entry, points of view and time frames as possible.

Here's one:

> I entered the story quite late. Such is my lot as a secondary character and yet, without me, there is no happy ending. As it is, I passed the cottage every day and often spoke to the old woman. Brought her a rabbit now and again and once a duck that she made an excellent soup out of. We laughed over that meal for in preparing it she had not found all the shot, and I had to repeatedly spit lead onto the floor as I ate. After that it was not unusual for me to stop and see how she was doing.

> What was unusual was that the door was open. Once inside, I saw that where the old woman should have been there was a great gray wolf sprawled on her bed in a tangle of torn sheets. *Meine Gott*, such a belly. You would have thought she was going to deliver a half-grown bear. Even as the wolf slept, the belly moved and I had to confirm my own curiosity. If the old woman was swallowed, was she still alive?

It has always been the responsibility of the narrator to build upon what happens to tell us whether a character in a folk tale is happy or afraid, determined or grief-stricken in response to situations and actions.

In contemporary storytelling, especially personal stories, we have come to expect that the thoughts and feelings of the principal characters will be revealed. After all, most personal stories are about challenge and change in which the revelation of what is felt, thought, decided and acted upon is a substantial part of what the story is about.

Still the choices about what to reveal – and when – can make a difference between a story and a good story. Here I'll quote Mark Twain's admonition that "The difference between the almost right word and the right word is really a large matter – it's the difference between the lightning bug and the lightning."

The Arc of the Narrator in the Story

We seldom think about who is telling the story. Yet, nothing has more influence on how a story affects the reader than the feeling that the narrator has about the characters. The narrator's emotional relationship to the story frames the way in which the reader or listener comes to the story. I will go into this in detail in a later chapter of the permissions and limitations of first- and third-person voices. But for now, consider the example of a personal story about an adventure or misadventure you had a number of years ago. You are not the same person now as you were then and the question is how do you feel about the person you were then? Do you judge the person you were then as foolish or naive or admirable? If the essence of the story is about a lesson learned are you sympathetic to the difficulty of learning that lesson or contemptuous of how long it took or how hard it was?

Here is the start of a personal story:

When I was growing up in Albuquerque, New Mexico, I joined the Boy Scouts. It was what every boy in my school wanted to do because it meant we could go camping. I was more than willing to suffer what seemed like an endless series of tasks that had to be done before we actually left for the Pecos River country because I had been promised the thrill of tents under the stars and cast iron skillets over an open fire. It was worth the Saturday mornings spent carrying twenty pounds of advertising flyers that were to be affixed to screen doors in the heat of nondescript block after treeless block. It made the barking dogs that periodically lunged for those screen doors and once or twice actually broke through them worth the fright. It was worth the riding in the back of a pickup truck and being driven to some who-knows-where spot on the mesa and climbing out to be told that lunch was a five-mile walk that way. We were being toughened up for adventure.

Here is another one:

The Great Scoutmaster said, "It is good for boys to suffer. It makes a man of them."

The scoutmasters of my youth were mostly army combat vets who preferred action to explanation. If their eager charges wanted to go camping, they'd have to earn it. Earning it meant a Saturday morning delivering advertising flyers door to door in the newly constructed developments with instructions not to come back until the sack was empty. Water? Those boys could have water when they were done.

I never thought I was being played for a fool or worse, for a pack mule, but in hindsight, six weeks of trudging through one neighborhood after another did little more than give me blisters and a slope shoulder where the twenty pounds of closeout sale circulars lay in the rough canvas bag. The smart ones found a way to feign excuses offered by fathers or mothers who needed them for chores at home or to take trips to someplace, anyplace that required leaving early. Others would do as many blocks as the scoutmaster watched, then dump the contents of their sack in the first arroyo they came to and sit smoking cigarettes in the shade of the closest tree or adobe wall. I didn't have the wit or courage for that, and so I did what was asked of me.

In each of these examples, the core story remains the same. That as a boy scout I earned money to pay for camping trips delivering advertising flyers. In each, the point of view is first-person past tense but my feelings are not the same. The emotional arc I am choosing as the narrator about that activity shifts from a basically positive (even optimistic) view in the first to decidedly negative in the second. For example, the self-judgment of *"I never thought I was being played for a fool ..."* is the adult narrator's comment on his youthful naiveté.

Is one better than the other? The answer depends on my intent as a narrator. From an audience perspective, each one is a story set in the past about a particular experience I had as a youth. In the first, my concern is to introduce the world from a slightly nostalgic point of view. This happened, this was what I did. In the second, the adult narrator is making a judgment about the experience that colors how the audience hears the story. To achieve that effect I made specific choices about the descriptive language to carry the weight of the narrator's negative feelings.

Unreliable Narrators

A particular kind of story that appears in literature is told by an **unreliable narrator**. The question is why? Why are they telling the tale? What purpose does a narrator of questionable veracity serve? How do we know they are unreliable?

An unreliable narration may be characterized by the presence of exaggerations (tall tales as an example), contradictions, impossibilities (whether fantasy or failures of logic/common sense) or limited knowledge. As the narration proceeds, the questionable statements begin to mount up leading the audience to wonder whether the narrator can be trusted or what is the intent of these incongruous bits?

One of the functions of an unreliable narrator is to engage the audience in precisely this kind of questioning: What the story is really about? Why it is the story being told this way? What fallacy motivates the narrator's unreliability? At the moment the audience understands that the apparent interpretation may not be the whole story – or the "true" story – they become more deeply involved in assembling what they believe will be the whole truth. When they are proved right, they feel a tremendous sense of accomplishment. When they discover they are wrong, they begin to reassess how or why they did not get it. In both cases, the unreliable narrator has invited them to actively participate.

There are five frequently used types of unreliable narrator:

• **Exaggerators** – who adjust the facts or add to the circumstances of the tale or make their role "bigger" and more exciting. This is common in tall tales where the rule of thumb for construction is: true, probably true, probably not true, and improbable but we've come this far ...

Look, this story would be nothing without me. You can say that I am the villain but what would you have without one? A child brings a basket of so-so goodies to an ailing grandmother. You need a wolf. Not just a run-of-the-mill wolf, one who can huff and puff and ... Sorry, that's another of my greatest hits though the reporters got the ending wrong. I ate pig for days. I have great lungs, great ears and wonderful big eyes. Deep penetrating eyes that can hypnotize a weak-willed mortal. And this mouth! Why, there is no wolf in seven counties that has a mouth like mine. I could swallow a cake whole. Hell, I could swallow Grandma in a single gulp without dislocating my jaw if I had a mind to.

• **Madmen** – who are often unreliable in a tragic sense,

suffering from some form of mental illness, disassociation or delusion and not knowing they are wrong. They also represent a particular decision that, as the creator of the story, you must make as to whether their being "nuts" is obvious from the beginning or comes at a later point as part of a revelation or plot twist.

> It had to have that ending. Justice demanded it. Morality demanded it. He had to be made to suffer. He had made others suffer and the rule of an eye for an eye demanded the comeuppance. A wolf, like a capitalist, is ravenous. One wants flesh, the other a so-called return on investment. One swallows an ill old woman. The other simply works her to worn out and tosses her on the ash heap of history. Why shouldn't the workers rise up? Why shouldn't the woodsmen hunt down those despoilers of the earth and cut their bellies end to end? Let the bile flow. Shoot them. Hang them from branches to feed the starving birds. Drag the corpse into the town square and proclaim the end of profit. I would do that and I did. Found the wolf and slit him open, end to end. It felt good to finally see blood spilled.

• **The Clown** – This narrator does not take the story seriously and wants to make it more interesting, so they play with the conventions of the form or the audience's expectations. This form of unreliable narration is often presented by means of asides or the direct address to the audience in the digressive or meta-narrated plot forms.

When mother sent me to Grandmother's, I thought well what now? It didn't look like much of an adventure to me. I was thinking more along the lines of meeting a fairy prince and going to the other world. But no, this story has no fairies, no giants, nothing but the narrow path through the damned dark woods. I mean, wouldn't you like a bright-eyed, tanned and lithe-bodied fairy? Maybe I'll just add one as we go. Yes, why should you suffer hearing this as I have to suffer the dull bare bones of telling it? This is a stupid story, and if I can make it more interesting, you better believe I will.

• **The Innocent** – who simply is too young or inexperienced to be able to tell an accurate story. Think of Huckleberry Finn, who misinterprets the intentions of many other characters in the story while presenting the harsh facts of the narrative. The Innocent does not know what they are saying (at least not the whole truth of it). Therefore, the Innocent offers a version of the world that is unlikely to match what we know to be true.

There was always a smell at GaMa's house. When she was well, vegetable soup and bread baking, wood smoke and her smell. Mother said it was the perfume she liked but I thought it was the sugar and spice she always told me we were made of. I like sugar and spice. I like her cookies. That day when I came to the bedside, it was different. And when I saw GaMa she looked different ... But mother always told me not to stare. Maybe that's what happened when you got old.

• **The Liar** – who deliberately wants to mislead the audience, to obscure or withhold vital information for their own purposes or gain. In many instances this is the most difficult narrator to construct because of an essential dichotomy. On the one hand, the audience needs to have a sense that they are being lied to. On the other, the lie (or liar) cannot be so obvious as to insult them and make them want to stop listening or reading.

How can you say that I deserved what I got? She was of an age to consent, or at least that's what she said. I asked. When I said ... "the better to hear you," "the better to see you," "the better to hold you," those were not the only things I said. There was also "are you sure you want to share this bed with me?" I mean "the better to eat you" was a metaphor for, you know, oral stuff. It should have been obvious. She didn't object. She spread her legs as willingly as any. I might have been a little too eager but I never heard her say stop. ...

There are many reasons why they might be unreliable but the choice to use an unreliable narrator is first and foremost about creating a unique point of view that asks the audience to be engaged in determining what the real story is. Whether that decision is successful also depends on the nature of the story and can work well where the narrator's lack of knowledge or intent to misdirect adds texture to an otherwise familiar or dull story.

The Arc of the Audience With the Story

In particular kinds of stories, ghost stories or jokes as examples, the arc of the audience is critically important. After all, the writer or teller has to shape their emotional response to the story in order to achieve the intended effect of fright or laughter.

The emotional journey of the audience, from the beginning to the end of the story, matters every time. Your decisions (how the audience enters the story, what we ask them to feel about the characters, the narrative progression as we go along, and – most importantly – how we want them to feel at the end), are worthy of the same careful consideration as who is telling the story and what plot form you want to use. Though you have little control over how they will actually respond, your intention should be to move them to satisfaction in the experience of reading or hearing a well-told tale. True, but you also want to move them toward a recognition that the world they have visited has meaning and bears a relationship to their own.

There are **two elements** for the crafting of the emotional arc of the audience. One element is the choice of narrative progression itself. I have talked about the choices and elements of plot forms in detail in *The New Book of Plots* but let me take a few moments to speak to the larger issue now.

How we frame the development creates a mechanism for arranging the details of our narrative. In the traditional folk and fairy tale the most common plot form is the straight narrative in which A proceeds B and B is followed by C until we arrive at the end. If we think once again of Joseph Campbell's "hero's Journey," there is an invitation to a journey, followed by an exchange of some nature which demonstrates the hero or heroine's worthiness. Then there is a series of adventures in which the ultimate outcome grows in importance scene-by-scene until a final triumph is achieved and there is an appropriate resolution. It is very much A leads to B leads to the conclusion.

Most Western audiences intuitively recognize the pattern, as much from the sheer familiarity of it as from the directness of the progression. Within that directness, there is room for the audience to make an emotional connection to the characters and the situation. On an elemental level, we want to root for a hero and see a villain defeated. This is as true of *Star Wars* and *The Lord of the Rings* as it is of *Jack and the Beanstalk* or *Molly Whuppie*. Satisfaction comes with our providing not only an engaging progression but in savoring the "right" details through voice and description to let the audience fully inhabit that world.

Other familiar narrative forms include the flashback, revelation and parallel plots. Each has its strengths and weaknesses. In each case the form provides a blueprint to embed the details that engage the audience in the story's emotional arc; one that gives them the space to identify and match their own emotional connections to the story being told. Yet the plot form does not in itself make those connections. That is your job as the narrator.

Am I repeating myself? Yes, and for one simple reason – when we are telling a chosen story to an audience, our obligation to the story and the audience is to tell it well enough that the audience is able to enter that world seamlessly. Which brings me to the second element of crafting the audience's emotional arc.

How well has the writer/teller matched the story to the audience? This can be answered in this series of questions:

- Is the content of the story **appropriate** for the age of the audience?
- Is the subject matter or the way it is presented **suitable**?
- Will the audience understand the **time, place and culture** of the story?
- Is **the language itself** too complex or too simple, too academic or confusingly culturally specific?

Of the various versions of *Little Red Riding Hood* I am offering as examples, most are not suitable for children. I would reserve the first and second version of the story told from any point of view for older teens or adults. With those groups the presentation of the story as a metaphor for larger and more difficult issues is appropriate. To tell *Little Red Riding Hood* for children or in a mixed (family) setting, I might tell the more familiar Brothers Grimm version from the girl's or wolf's point of view but with a much lighter touch. Perhaps I might make fun of the conventions and logic (or lack of it) in the more familiar versions of the story, but in answering those four questions, I would deem the two oldest versions of the story inappropriate for children. The Brothers Grimm did as well, and changed the story to give it a wider appeal.

Even when I do want to push the boundaries of what is appropriate for an audience or explore how much trust they have in me as a teller, I want to find the narrow path between making the familiar lively and subverting audience expectations that a particular story can only be told in one way. My choice of plot form and narrator can open up what they think a story is to a new understanding of what it can be.

Judgment and Truth

Another question might be: Is the audience willing to hear what the story offers? This brings us to a moment of consideration of judgment and truth in the emotional arc of stories. This is particularly a consideration in our telling difficult or personal stories.

There are many venues where stories are told: festivals, theaters, showcases, story slams, churches, schools, libraries and more. In the last two decades, with the emergence of the Moth and other story slams, open mic or curated venues, there has been a rise in the telling of "true" intimate or difficult personal stories. Those stories are not always easy to tell or comfortable to hear though they often present a compelling emotional immediacy.

The truth of a story does not reside in its emotional rawness. Often they seem more like a kind of therapy that the unwitting audience is asked to witness than a crafted story of an understood and resolved emotion or experience. That does not mean such stories cannot or should not be told, but I think there is an ethical consideration about when and how we tell them ... And which audiences are appropriate for those stories.

Certainly, we should not tell a story that is not understood, resolved or crafted for public presentation. That is an invitation to emotionally trigger either the teller or the audience. That **unresolved material** should be shared with a therapist, support group or intimate friends. As the old joke goes,

> The difference between therapy and storytelling is that in therapy the teller pays the audience.

When a story is understood and consciously crafted and *the audience knows that there is a probability of hearing difficult material*, there is no issue for the storyteller other than finding the best way to convey the material. On the part of the audience, the only decision is whether to stay or leave.

In what some call "the homogeneity of political correctness," there has been heated conversation about "triggers" and how the narrator should warn and/or prepare the audience for potentially troubling material. Some are of the opinion that one should not tell material that can trigger emotional trauma, while others feel that as long as it is contextualized, it's appropriate. This is probably an individual decision that should be based upon both the content of the narrative and the context of the sharing. This goes back to the fundamental idea that there is an **unspoken but assumed contract** between the writer/teller and the audience that each will offer the other trust and permission for the sake of the story.

Having thought about, written about, told and taught difficult stories for four decades now, I take the position that **respect for the audience** does matter. I would not tell particular kinds of stories to families or in general entertainment venues. There are times when I will modify stories and provide contexts for an audience, but my preference is to leave the difficult and adult material for performance in Fringe Festival, cabaret, support group and adult venues where the audience is choosing to hear about troubled lives and R or X-rated material.

Exercises in Developing Narrative Arcs:

Exercise 1: Working the larger narrative arc – how does the story move? Tell the story with a rising (cumulative) emotional narrative – fear, confusion or delight. Pay attention to the details of sensory imagery, pacing and the choice of a supportive narrative plot. Tell a small story that reflects those choices. (5 minutes) Discuss the experience and the choices. What does your listener hear as engaging and supportive of those choices? (5 minutes)

Exercise 2: Working the narrator's arc – who is telling this story and what do they know? If you can only tell what you know to be your thoughts, feelings or motivations when you tell in the first person, how does the choice of present or past tense affect the narrative? Choose one and tell the story. (5 minutes) Discuss the experience. (5 minutes) Repeat the story from the other time frame. (5 minutes) What are the differences? What does the audience want or need from each?

Tell this story using an unreliable narrator. What methods do you use to indicate that choice to the audience? Pay attention to the tension between what is said and what is unsaid in the story. Tell that story. (5 minutes) Discuss the experience. (5 minutes)

Exercise 3: Working the audience arc – consider the function of details and the conditions of performance.

What do you do to reinforce or subvert expectations based upon the genre or story type? Discuss your choices paying attention to the usual conventions of the story type. Now tell a story. (5 minutes) What did your audience experience? What worked for them? What didn't? What more do they want?

Chapter Three
How Much Is Needed to Make the World?

First and foremost, to make the world the characters live in and the audience can enter requires details that only the storyteller knows. Whenever I have taught storytelling, I have always said that *the function of the storyteller is to know MORE than they tell.* There are two clear values in this. The first is that it lets you select the appropriate details for the audience you are sharing the story with. This is especially true for oral performance where the constraints of time, the mix of audience age and culture may require you to trim or add material to a story to increase their understanding and enjoyment of the tale. The second is that it lets you make a selection of what you tell and when in order to effectively frame the emotional arcs of the story.

That the storyteller knows more than he tells is obvious in the personal story. By its very nature, a personal story is a piece of your life. You have to decide where to begin and where to end. Both of those points are abutting other pieces of your life that may affect how you feel about the material you are telling or what you should include. You can't tell everything and, more importantly, you shouldn't. Remember, a story is a **chosen narrative** crafted to serve a purpose for an intended audience. What you tell around the family table, to your therapist or to people who have paid good money to sit in uncomfortable chairs and be entertained should not be the same thing.

The question is always what details does a specific audience know or need to know? The obvious answer is that they need to know enough to follow the story. In *The Three Little Pigs*, as an example, they need to know there are three pigs, three houses and a wolf. That's the bare bones of it. But to give the story texture, *you have many choices* available to you. You can add descriptions of the time and place. You can describe the straw, wood and brick houses in greater or lesser detail. You can distinguish between the pigs by their appearances, how they speak (if they do) and how they perform their specific actions within the narrative frame. The same can be done with the wolf who can be sly or aggressive, opportunistic or stupid, or as the real victim of this tale. (The wolf has, in fact, been portrayed in each of those ways in different versions of the story.)

Here are three examples of details for *Little Red Riding Hood* that provide too few, too many and close to "just enough" detail:

> Once upon a time, there was a sweet little girl. Everyone who saw her liked her, but most of all her grandmother, who did not know what to give the child next. Once she gave her a little cap made of red velvet. Because it suited her so well, and she wanted to wear it all the time, she came to be known as Little Red Cap.

> One day her mother said to her, "Come Little Red Cap. Here is a piece of cake and a bottle of wine. Take them to your grandmother. She is sick and weak, and they will do her well. Mind your manners and give her my greetings. Behave yourself on the way, and do not leave the path, or you might fall down and break the glass, and then there will be nothing for your grandmother. And when you enter her parlor, don't forget to say 'good morning,' and don't peer into all the corners first."

> "I'll do everything just right," said Little Red Cap, shaking her mother's hand.

The grandmother lived out in the woods, a half-hour from the village. When Little Red Cap entered the woods a wolf came up to her. She did not know what a wicked animal he was, and was not afraid of him. (The Brothers Grimm text)

Yes, though that example is Jacob and Wilhelm Grimm's "original" text, it is pretty sparse on detail and heavy on plot progression. It could use more description to help us see the characters and place where they reside but there is little value in adding material willy-nilly and going to the other extreme of overloading it.

Once upon a time, there was a sugar-sweet little girl. She was bright and kind to man and beast which would be her downfall. Everyone who saw her liked her, but most of all her frail grandmother, who did not know what to give the child next. No gift was too much. One shiny toy after another was offered, used and discarded.

Once she gave her a little cap made of red velvet that framed her innocent face and dark curls. Because it suited her so well, and she wanted to wear it all the time, she came to be known as Little Red Cap.

One day her very strict and too often judgmental mother said to her, "Come, Little Red Cap, I have a chore for you. Here is a piece of German chocolate cake and a bottle of Spanish red wine for health. Take them to that doting grandmother of yours who spoils you in ways that will give you false expectations making you dependent on the kindness of others. She is sick and weak, and though she sometimes drinks too much, they will do her well. Mind your manners, Little Miss, and give her my greetings. Behave yourself on the way, and do not leave the path. You might get lost since you are easily distracted. You might fall down and break the glass, and then there will be nothing for your grand-mother and that would be your fault. I don't want to hear that you misbehaved or I'll give you a switching.

"And let me tell you girl, that when you enter her parlor, don't forget to say 'good morning,' and don't peer into all the corners first. If you can remember to do it, you should wash the old lady's dishes and sweep the hearth because I'm sure that she hasn't done any since she's taken ill."

"I'll do everything just right," said Little Red Cap, taking her mother's calloused hand. "I'll show you that I am a big girl now."

The grandmother lived at the edge of a small clearing in the dark woods in a little thatch cottage with morning glories growing around the sturdy door. Small as it was, the cottage was cluttered with herbs and potions and all the things that made half the town think that she was a witch and the rest seek her out for remedies for their every ache and pain. It was but a half hour from the village if you stayed on the well-worn path.

No sooner than a nervous Little Red Cap entered the woods when a large gray wolf came up to her. He smiled in a vaguely friendly way. She did not know what a wicked animal he was, and thinking herself brave, pretended she was not afraid of him though she should have been if she had the sense that God gave a doorknob.

There is so much extraneous detail in this example that it comes close to pushing the audience (and me as the teller) out of the story as I get stuck on wondering about one choice after another. There is also a problem in that much of the detailing is not about an appeal to the senses but is judgmental description, essentially making the third person point of view an attempt to bias the audience against the heroine.

So here is a third version with what might be "just enough" detail.

Once upon a time, there was a sweet little girl. She was

kind to everyone she met. Everyone who saw her liked her, but most of all her grandmother, who spoiled her to the point where she did not know what to give the child next. She gave her a little cap made of red velvet that framed her innocent face and blond curls. Because it suited her so well, and the child wanted to wear it all the time, she came to be known as Little Red Cap.

One day her mother said to her, "Come Little Red Cap. Here is a piece of German chocolate cake and a bottle of red wine. Take them to your grandmother who is sick and weak, and they will help her recover. Mind your manners and give her my greetings. Behave yourself on the way, and do not leave the well-worn path. You might fall down and break the glass, and then there will be nothing for your grandmother. When you enter her parlor, don't forget to say 'good morning,' and don't peer into all the corners first."

"I'll do everything just as you desire," said Little Red Cap.

The grandmother lived out in the dark woods, a half hour from the village at the edge of the well-worn path. When Little Red Cap entered the woods a great gray wolf came up to her. She did not know what a wicked animal he was, and was not afraid of him.

Why is this just right? First of all the details largely **appeal to the senses** - how things look, sound, smell, taste or feel, Red Riding Hood has curls of a particular color. The cake is German chocolate. The forest is dark. The path is well worn. The wolf is gray. Each of these is specific and will help the audience fill in the picture.

The Universal and the Particular

One of the best tools for deciding what details should be used is to consider the role of images and themes in a story. Those two aspects are also a mechanism for understanding and arriving at the universal and the particular in crafting stories.

I am indebted again to Nancy Donoval for refining our approach to images and themes over our years of teaching together.

Let's begin with a variation of the definition of what a story is. A story is a set of chosen and shaped images recreating an event or series of events, real or fictitious, in which meaning, change or insight occur. Again, it is not simply a matter of relating the plot when we are crafting an event or series of events. The story needs concrete Images and universal themes to enable it to carry meaning, present change or offer insight.

A story's images exist in specific moments of time and place. This is what keeps the story from simply being a polemic or incoherent ramble. Concrete images engage the mind making the story REAL to the audience's imagination. **Concrete images** can be thought of as the "outside" details of the story that include:

- Looks
- Sounds
- Smells
- Tastes
- Feels to the touch/texture
- Physical movement within the story

Universal themes engage the heart making the story MATTER emotionally to the audience. They can be thought of as the "inside" support for the story to illuminate or explore the fundamental aspect(s) of being human. The theme speaks to what the story is about that is more than just its events. Themes can identify or call out the conflicts or opposing forces (internal as well as external) that are in the story. At this point, Nancy would caution that you want to use care so that your theme supports the story and does not to become the story. And I would concur.

Here are some specific questions to help get at themes:

- What or who changes?
- What relationships (between which characters) drive the story?
- What choices do characters make? Why those choices?
- What are the consequences of those choices?
- How do the characters feel about what they do or what happens? Why?
- How do you *(as the author/narrator)* feel about what happens?
- Why are you telling *this* story to *this* audience?

A story can have a number of themes within it but it's important for the storyteller to know what the core of the story is, what the writer or storyteller intends the story to be about *beyond what happens.*

Here is a personal story example:

One summer when I was growing up in Albuquerque, New Mexico, we did a lot of what we kids called Indian wrestling. It was the game played while you waited for other kids, or between the larger and longer games of baseball, football or hide-n-seek. It was played out of the view of parents who would yell at you for getting grass stains on your clothes. The rules were simple: two people lay on the ground, side by side facing different directions, their elbows crooked and arms interlocking. On the count of three, they would raise the leg closest to their opponent and try to catch the other person's leg and force it down. Up, grab, down. The stronger force would break their grip and send the weaker tumbling.

Most of the kids who participated were pretty well matched for height and weight. Consequently, it was a game in which speed counted as much as brute strength. A small boy, or even a girl, if they were fast enough could roll backward as their leg came up and then by rocking forward use the momentum to overpower a larger or slower playmate.

Being a game in which there was rough equality, it seldom produced consistent winners. Often the same two opponents would challenge each other over and over again: legs flashing up, bodies tumbling with laughter, to immediately jump back down to try again, until they were simply too tired or dizzy to continue.

In retrospect, what seems unusual now was then unquestioned: in that brief interlude between sixth and seventh grade, both boys and girls participated. For most of us, it would be another year before we had that growth spurt that declared the separation of jocks from nerds, the fat from thin, men from women. And though a few of the girls had begun to wear training bras, consciousness of sexuality was still largely nascent and confused.

After supper one night, a rumor swept the block that there was still time for a ball game so we rode our bikes over to Tony Alverez's house. Four or five guys were there. A few of the neighbor girls seeing Tony had company came over. Lucy Trejo was with them, but unlike the others in their shorts and sweatshirts, she was wearing a yellow sundress.

While we waited to see who else would come, Tony challenged Tommy Unkovich to a match. Tommy wasn't big, but he was a strong kid, sure of himself. Tony was slightly larger, cocky and quick. One, two, three. Tommy sent Tony sailing halfway across the yard.

Again. Again. Four, five, six times.

Each time Tony came back angrier than before. Tommy sensing the potential *for trouble or perhaps just losing interest got up and started to walk away.*

Lucy said a few things about Tony's inability to budge Tommy. Tony grabbed Tommy, demanding to go again.

Tommy declined and said Tony should try someone else, me or my brother, or Donny Smith. Or since he couldn't seem to beat a little guy, maybe he should wrestle big-mouthed Lucy.

Tony wheeled around red-faced, looking for a challenge. We avoided eye contact. Then he looked at her and she stepped forward, telling him that *even she could send him flying.*

He fell to the ground. She kicked off her sandals and lay down beside him. There was a tension in the air, not just one of challenge and anger, but something else, something unnamed. Her sundress had slid up her legs, and I felt an awkward discomfort looking at her white cotton panties and those long skinny legs. She and Tony were breathing hard, neither saying a thing.

One, two, three. Their legs came up and locked, but neither seemed to be able to throw the other. They rocked back and forth like flipped over turtles, their legs waving in the air and their heads straining to see over their bellies. Then she laughed and brought her leg down. Tony tumbled away from her.

He sprang to his feet and jumped on top of Lucy, sitting down hard on her belly, his legs straddling her body.

His hand formed a fist and he struck at her, but she caught his wrist in her hand before he could land the blow. The girls began to scream. Donny went to pull Tony off but the two of them rolled away from us, across the lawn, grunting and kicking.

When they came to a stop, she was straddling him, holding his arms down. Her sundress was ripped, falling away from one shoulder. She sat back, firmly planting her butt against his waist and then leaned down and kissed him on the mouth, hard. We could see Tony jerk under her and go suddenly limp like he had received an electrical shock.

That's when the grown-ups came running out of the house. Tony's mother grabbed Lucy around the waist, pulling her off, with Lucy kicking at Tony as she was hauled up and away. Tony's father, yelling something in Spanish, got a handful of Tony's hair and jerked him to his feet. Mr. Alverez began to swat Tony with a rolled-up newspaper, driving him into the house with a rain of blows like he was a misbehaving dog.

Lucy stood there sobbing, then turned her back on the gathering and ran home.

Everyone knew there would be hell to pay for what

had happened, but I saw from the wide-eyed stares of the boys gripping the handlebars of their bikes that we weren't sure what had happened. No one said anything. There would be no ball game tonight. We got on our bikes and went home. Indian wrestling would be put aside for a while and when it was taken up again, the girls never played.

So let's begin with images. What are they? They could include:

> How the game was played.
> Lucy in a yellow sundress.
> Tommy defeating Tony.
> The discomfort of seeing Lucy's panties when her
> sundress slips up.
> Tony on top of Lucy.
> Lucy on top of Tony.
> Her kissing him.
> Tony's father with a rolled-up newspaper.
> Riding bikes home.

What other concrete images, especially ones that reference the senses or movement does this story suggest to you?

Then let's look at what might be the themes. They could include:

Childhood games.

Waiting for something to happen.

Pride goes before the fall.

Nascent sexuality.

Confusion.

Loss of innocence.

The separation of the sexes.

What other themes that reference being human does this story suggest to you? It may be helpful for you to go back to the questions of who or what or changes in the story and what relationships are driving the story to see if there are additional themes for this story.

When I created this story, I began with a specific memory. After I thought about what had happened in the most literal sense of what was the event, I made a note to myself that there are kids (and adults) who did not play this game so I would have to build a description of what it was into the front of the story. Then I looked at what was needed image-by-image to convey what I wanted the story to do. What I wanted it to do was to make the often-uncomfortable space between childhood and being a teen visible.

At that point, I told two variations of this story a few times with different audiences to see what they heard and felt.

Think of this as your research and development phase. This was the point where I began to look at the themes I saw and those the audience saw. Two related themes – nascent sexuality and confusion – emerged as the themes where the audience felt the most engagement. That was what I would more fully and carefully develop.

Let me be clear, some audience members felt discomfort with either version of the story as it stood and others wanted clearer images for those themes. I can live with some members of the audience being uncomfortable because *the point of my telling this story* is to explore that **moment when the world shifts**. It is an uncomfortable moment and one many adults would rather not talk about or even acknowledge. It is also a moment that is helpful for pre-teens and teens to hear. An experience they may not have specifically had, but one that points to feelings they may have had.

I then added the image of my response to Lucy's sundress slipping up and her crying. I don't remember if either of those things happened in the actual historical event. Tommy and Tony's exchange, Lucy defeating Tony and his reaction, Tony's father with the newspaper – those things happened. Yet, without adding a few more details, those more difficult themes of the story remained undeveloped. I wanted to bring the images and narrative into alignment with what the audience had the strongest connection to.

Adding those details – and the last image of kids trying to figure out what had happened – accomplished that end.

The whole of the story begins with a fact. Throughout, the use of specific images underlines the themes and (potential) meaning.

It is the interplay of images and themes that creates the lovely paradox of the **Universal found in the Particular**. To make the point, I'll paraphrase Joseph Stalin saying, "A million deaths is a statistic, one death is a tragedy." The statistic is universal but carries little emotional meaning. The singular is the particular, the specific that allows us to feel the tragedy. Six million dead in the Holocaust, 100 years of lynching in the South – for many people these are too large to comprehend except as abstractions, but the story of one Jew, Yvonne Engelmann, who survived the gas chamber in Auschwitz or one 14-year-old black boy, Charlie Lang, taken from a Mississippi jail by a white mob and hung are tragic stories. They can be understood as the specific experience of another human being in a world of larger meaning.

There are applications of the Universal and Particular, of themes and images that go beyond the traditional or personal story. When I am working in that portion of my storytelling that is the political advocacy and message framing work, I always work with my client organizations and groups to try to find the particular metaphor or emotionally latent story that makes challenges, issues and statistics "real" for politicians and policymakers. Just as I did with our sample story, I look for a narrative that can carry specific images and significant themes that invite an understanding of the complex, of the universal issue in a particular and human story.

When a low-wealth advocacy group in northern Minnesota wanted to develop a message about poverty and transportation issues, the stories told were variations on cars not working when they needed to and money not available to repair them. From those stories they were able to pick **one particular story** that touched every aspect of fact and feeling and could be told easily. More than that they developed a message – "We want to work, help us get there." – that conveyed the universal of their issue and the response they wanted from the local government simply and directly. Using the message whenever they could, they would follow it with the particular human story of how getting to work was frustrating and what kinds of help would let them be productive citizens.

Section Two
The Power of Point of View

Chapter Four
Three Voices in the Now and Then

Now it is time to look at the development of character and cultural voice. They are manifest in the point of view, with choices of first-, second- or third-person narrative and usually in one of two fundamental time frames – present or past tense – as our building blocks.

Here is the fundamental chart of characteristics:

	Present	Past
First person	Can only know what they know as an individual at this moment.	Knows what happened and how they feel/felt about what happened.
Second person	Is addressing a particular other and only knows what has transpired up to this moment.	Is addressing a particular person and to some degree the why or how of their past actions or emotions.
Third person	The universal narrator who knows what everyone is doing, feeling, and the why or how of what any character knows in the moment.	The universal narrator who knows what everyone felt or did at every point in the story.

First Person

The first person point of view is the most familiar to us. It is the "I" that we use for our own stories. It is my narrative with any and all the choices I make to tell those stories. Generally, they are told in the past tense, as something that happened before this moment and may or may not include lessons learned, "morals" or punch lines. They are told to someone – family, friends, those we work with – and often presume that they know us and our history and geography well enough for us to use a kind of shorthand of not explaining every player or every nuance of setting.

We don't often think about who we are telling that story to and don't consciously craft the story except through the repetition of telling it to others. Yet craft them we do and over time our memory conforms to the particular version we have revised over time based on the responses from those we have told them to. This is why two brothers can have the same experience such as playing baseball together and over the course of years wind up telling stories that begin with the same general experience but differ, perhaps in significant ways, in the details and focus. Each brother assumes that the "I" of their first person, past tense, is true to the facts. While the likelihood is that either version may be true to the emotional facts, but not necessarily true to the external facts a third party might offer having observed both brothers in the situation being retold.

First Person/Past Tense

The defining characteristics of the first person/past tense are that the narrator knows what happened *from their perspective*, how *they feel/felt* about it, *what they learned or didn't*, and the kinds of connections they made between X and Y. This kind of narrative is often abbreviated with the elements of

- The narrative progression of *what happened.*
- The emotional response *in the moment* it happened as recounted after the moment.
- The kind of *detail* particular to the nature of the story and the teller.

How much of each is offered in the story is entirely relational to the audience and whether the teller wants to present themselves as a hero, fool or something else. Some tellers only focus on what happened or how they felt moment to moment in a particular situation. Some are telling the story to set up a joke at their own or someone else's expense. Again this is driven by both habit (how they prefer to tell an "I" story) and their relationship to the particular audience who may ask questions or interrupt in hopes that they can move the storyteller to telling it more to their liking, which usually means to tell it more the way they would tell it.

Here is our example of first person/past tense:

I told you the other day how it got started what with mother telling me to take a basket to my Grandma's house. And I probably told you that I met someone in the woods but then mother came into the room and I had to skip the rest of the story. She'd find it too disturbing. I mean when I got home she asked how Grandma was and I tried to brush it off. I said she was sleeping. I mean I didn't want to say she was dead. She was, of course. He had killed her but I didn't know that when I got to the house.

I knocked on the door and it just swung open. Creepy but there's lots of things at her house that are. Bunches of flowers hanging from the rafters, glass jars with animal parts and icky stuff in them that she says she uses for her medicine. I went in and it's dark. The bedroom light was on, so I took off my red cloak and left it with the basket on the table and went into the bedroom to see how sick she was. She was in bed, the covers up and some stupid looking hat pulled down so low I could barely see her eyes. It smelled funny. Not that old person smell but something else, more like some guy's aftershave.

When I sat on the edge of the bed, she spoke to me but it didn't sound much like her. Here's the part that freaks me out. He was wearing her clothes! It was the guy in the woods. He was in her bed wearing her flannel nightgown and when I got up to go away because it wasn't anywhere close to right, he jumped out from under the covers and grabbed me. Pulled my clothes off.

Well not everything, just the bottoms and pinned me to the bed. I was yelling and wiggling and he's pressing me down. And his thing, you know, that thing is huge and hard, and he's trying to stick it between my legs. Gross.

It hurt. There was blood and stuff. I wanted to pee right there on the bed. But he was still grabbing me and rubbing his whiskers on my face, and licking me. Double gross. Finally, he kind of slid off me and I said I wanted to go pee. He looked at me like he had never heard someone say that before. Then he laughed and took a rope from beneath the bed – what the hell was that doing there? Tie me up? Well, he did, sort of. He tied the rope around my ankle and said that when he tugged I had to come back. Or what? Or he'd be really mad and I'd wind up like Grandma. That's when he told me that he had strangled her.

I didn't want to be strangled. I didn't want him to do what it was he tried to do again, so I went out of the room and ducked behind the counter. It was easy to untie the rope 'cause he had made a shitty knot. I made a good one around the leg of the stool that Grandma used to sit on when she was making potions. Then I grabbed my red cloak from the table, crawled over to the door and slipped out. No, I didn't have my pants. I wasn't going to go back there to try to get them.

I just wrapped myself in the cloak and ran home. Lucky for me, mother wasn't in the house when I got there, so I could wash myself and put on another bottom before she came back from the market.

I wondered if I should tell her anything or if she'd figure out something had happened. She didn't ask anything other than did I leave the basket for Granny and I said, yes. The rest is my secret and yours. You have to swear you won't say anything to anybody. I need time to figure out what to do. Maybe I'll get a gun and shoot him. Maybe I'll get Joey, you know the cute guy who cuts wood, and see if he wants to do something about the creep for me.

First Person/Present Tense

The essential feature of first person/present tense is that the "I" who is narrating the story can only know what they know as an individual at this particular moment. While they know the past they are not privy to the future or what any other character thinks or feels unless that character reveals it. The story is theirs alone.

Why use it then?

Central to this voice is emotional immediacy and uncertainty of outcome. This is the voice of crisis and action. What do I feel right now? What are my choices right now? This point of view can easily and necessarily be a keen observer of internal and external detail in the moment.

And here is the same example moved from past to present tense:

1. Mother is telling me to take a basket to my Grandma's house and of course I'll say yes. A walk through the woods, a visit with the Grandmother who loves me. Won't that be fun?

2. I'm knocking on the door when it swings open. Creepy but there's lots of things at her house that are. Bunches of flowers hanging from the rafters, glass jars with animal parts and icky stuff in them that she says she uses for her medicine. It's dark but I might as well go in. The bedroom light is on, so I'll take off my red cloak and leave it with the basket on the table.

3. Grandma is in bed with the covers up and some stupid looking hat pulled down so low I can barely see her eyes. It smells funny. Not that old person

smell but something else, more like some guy's aftershave.

Sitting on the edge of the bed, she speaks to me but it doesn't sound much like her. She's hoarse or something, and so soft I'll have to lean closer to hear her.

4. Dear God, that isn't Grandma. He's wearing her clothes! The guy in the woods, he's here in her bed, wearing her flannel nightgown. Time to go. This isn't anywhere close to right ... No, no, don't touch me. Leave me alone. He's pulling my bottoms off. Ouch, he's strong. The more I struggle the more he's pressing me down. I try kicking him but he catches my leg and is forcing it – no, I'll try to keep my knees together. His breath is terrible. His thing is huge and hard and he's trying to stick it between my legs. Gross. I can't look. Not at that, not at his face, not at anything but the wall.

5. It hurts. There is blood and stuff. I want to pee right here on the bed. He is still grabbing me, rubbing his whiskers on my face and licking me.

6. I have to go pee. He's looking at me like he's never heard someone say that before. He laughs and is

taking a rope from beneath the bed – what the hell is that doing there? Does he want to tie me up? The rope goes around my ankle and he says that when he tugs I'd better come back. Or what? Or he'll be really mad and I'll wind up like Grandma. Oh my God, she's dead. He's strangled her.

I don't want to be strangled. I don't want him to do that thing again, so now that I'm out of the room, I'm going to leave. Duck behind the counter. Untie the rope 'cause he had made a shitty knot. I'll make a good one right here around the leg of the stool that Grandma uses when she makes potions. Tug on that, you hairy beast. I'll grab my red cloak from the table, crawl to the door and slip out. I don't have my pants, but I'm not going to go back there to try to get them. I'll figure out what to say about not having them later.

7. Lucky for me mother isn't in the house, so I can wash myself and put on another bottom before she comes back from the market. What can I say? That I've been attacked? That her darling daughter is ruined?

I need time to figure out what to do, Maybe, I'll get a gun and shoot him. Maybe I'll get Joey, the cute guy who cuts wood to do something about the creep for me. Joey likes me. He'll be pissed that he wasn't the first but if he really likes me, he'll help me even the score.

You'll notice that there is a problem in writing in the first person/present tense: how to construct the progression of the narrative so that the reader/hearer arrives at the end without reverting to the past tense or confusing the reader/audience. Writing this moment, and then the next moment, and the one that comes after it – *all in the present tense* can be frustrating if we do not have ways of distinguishing between one **now** and another. The easiest answer is to write vignettes, specific and discrete bits of imagery or dialogue that exist in a specific present. Then you, the writer or teller, must separate those vignettes in some way that the reader or listener understands as moving from one to another.

A second answer to the problem is to introduce more than one character narrating in that present tense, and changing points-of-view as the action develops. This is one of the uses of the parallel plot form.

As an example, *Little Red Riding Hood* may be narrated in the present tense A) the girl talking about being in the woods, B) then the wolf on meeting her, C) then Red on the joy of picking flowers, D) then Grandma on the arrival of a visitor, and so on, in whatever sequence of present moments best suits the needs of the story from each character's first-person, present-tense voice.

Here's an abbreviated version of what that specific sequence for *Little Red Riding Hood* would look like:

> I always have feelings about the forest. It's so large and dark, I can barely see my way from the edge of town to Grandma's. I know the sun is shining and those moments when it breaks through the tangle of branches and leaves, the bright light is shocking. Each warm moment that illuminates the path is like a tiny island of comfort.

> I can smell the goodies in the wicker basket – chocolate, bread and beer. No, not bread, it's a cake. A German chocolate cake and not beer, an elderberry wine so red it is almost purple. I should have recognized them at first sniff but the first sniff was not what was in the basket but the one carrying it. She is small, delicate perhaps though it is hard to tell with that ridiculous red cloak. She moves like a fawn and I'll bet that she tastes like one as well, tender flesh ready to be tasted.

It was a lovely suggestion to pick some flowers. There are so many of them here in the meadow. I'm sure Gran'mama will like these – wild daisies with paper-white petals curved as if they were sculpted by a sure hand, Queen Anne's lace and there, at the edge of the wood, wild roses with tiny blossoms and hips she can use for tea when the petals have shed their fragrance.

Who is that at the door? I'm not expecting anyone. Perhaps it is the woodsman come to visit. I haven't seen him in too long. I'm too weak to get out of this welcome bed, the strain of walking to greet them will shorten my breath and bend me over in pain. I'll call out "come in" and they can sit here beside me. Let them tell me of the world and if they are a good guest and have a bit of something to drink, we can lift a glass to good fortune.

Exercises for the Development of the First-Person Point of View

1. Take any traditional story that you know well and select a character. It can be the central character (hero or

heroine, villain) or a secondary character. Have them tell the story in their voice. Use the first person/past tense including these three elements in that narration:

- Something about who they are – background and how they came to be where they are doing what they do.
- Something about their awareness of sensory responses – how something looked, sounded, smelled, tasted or felt – that prompted them to make a discovery or act.
- Something about how they felt – excitement, fear, joy – at a particular moment in the story.

What do you include? Ask yourself how each element adds to the progression of the story. Remember for the purposes of this exercise everything in the story should contribute to the whole. What is needed? What is too much and can be left out? Tell it.

2. Now select another character from that same story and tell it from their first-person/past-tense point of view. Use the same criteria. How does the story change? What is unique to their experience? Tell it.

3. Select a specific event or moment in your own life. It does not need to be a moment of crisis though often

the experience of an accident works well for this exercise. Tell that moment in the first person/present tense. Begin by describing where and when you are. Describe the **where** in as much detail as possible. Identify your **emotion** at the start of the event. What is the first awareness that something is happening? Describe what that is from the first moment to its completion. Describe any emotions you have in the moment. Describe what you think as it happens. Look at everything you have described and decide on an order. Assume that in the present, time expands and you have the luxury of focusing on several things at once, even if you describe them in a sequence. Do you need to start with the where and when or with some other detail? Tell it.

Second Person

The second person is not used often for it represents a difficult challenge. It is a narration addressed to "you" with the audience standing in for the one being addressed. Who is the "you" being spoken to? It is in many ways a sleight of hand, in which the story is framed from the actions and motivations of the "you" being addressed but the story is actually being told by another party who may, or may not, be clearly identified. This is both the thrill and the difficulty of this point of view. The audience, whether hearing or reading this, must understand who the "you" is and be willing to suspend their judgment about that role being assigned them long enough to enter the story. Is the audience being asked to be Red Riding Hood, the Wolf or someone else with particular knowledge or a central role in the story?

It is the obligation of the narrator to provide **enough** information that the audience can understand who is being addressed and **not so much** that the audience anticipates what comes next. The choice of this form of narrative, whether in the present or past tense, will require some mix of **details and surprises** that keep the audience engaged and wanting to hear what comes next.

For all the difficulty in crafting this point of view, it does allow significant permission to ascribe motives and behavior to the "you" being addressed. This is one place where an unreliable narrator can reign because the essence of their narration is not about themselves but about what they think the subject of their narrative feels or does, whether there is a factual basis for it or not. This is a narration in which gossip, imagination and projection can have a free hand.

Here is **second person, present tense,** which is perhaps the most difficult of all of these to sustain:

You claim to be the hero of the story, but on what basis? That you come into the story with your axe and your attitude after my supposed wickedness is done. Who are you to say that I am the villain of the piece? Do you stop to think for one moment, that I'm doing what comes naturally or that the old woman didn't think it was a relief to be finished with this poverty and pain crap?

Don't start with, "If I'm playing my role as the predator; you're just playing yours ... As what? You're not Superman. You're a convenience. Let me remind you that in every previous version of this story you don't even show up. Why are you here at all? Because those Germans think that their sense of virtue or injury needs to be rectified? Justice? What kind of justice is it for you to split me open and stuff rocks in my belly? That's not justice, that's sadism.

"If this is about saving the child, why are you waiting until after I've finished off my meal, why didn't you show up before we went through that cloying dialogue about what big things I have? That would have been a good time for you and I to go mano a mano and to see what big things I do have and what kind of a hero you really are. But here you are late to the ball, all anxious to be the one who saves the girl. My bad luck and for what?

You don't get her. You'll do me in and the dammed story will be over."

Yes, there is not a lot of action in this example of second person, present tense. It is mostly talking but what is happening is significant. The **direct address** to the other allows the narrator to focus not so much on what happens as the **why**. The difficulty will be the same as in the first person, present tense: how will you segment the narrative to move the story forward? Again the use of vignettes or multiple characters narrating (though they may not and probably should not all be in second person, present tense) is a way to achieve the plot progression.

I will also point out that in this example that the "you" being addressed (the hunter/woodsman) is clearly indicated in the second sentence by the (actual) narrator (the wolf) within the story. As soon as the audience understands that the woodsman is the "you" they can enjoy the antagonism between the narrator and the subject of the narration.

Here is an example of second person, past tense in which the roles are reversed:

"You certainly were the villain in this story, my hairy antagonist. You always are and as much as you might want to argue that it is prejudice, having been cast in the role you more than lived up to it. Right from the start, your intentions are deceitful. You asked the girl what is in the basket and where she's going. You decided then and there to take advantage of her by suggesting that she should leave the path to pick flowers. You could have simply grabbed the basket and ran but no, in that wicked heart of yours you decided to go to Grandma's, dispatch the old lady and lay in wait. You had no guilt or shame, no remorse for your actions. You put on her nightgown and snuggled under the covers in hopes of fooling the child. Sick. For what terrible purpose did you lay in wait in the bedroom shadows? To satisfy your base urges by swallowing an innocent child whole. Your villainy is obvious and deserving of the punishment you received, your greed so complete that you didn't even chew. Glutton. In that you defeated your own purpose and with the stoke of my blade she sprang out of your opened belly still living."

I imagine that you still might wonder, *why bother with this point of view?* Present tense, past tense, it seems quite difficult in its construction and of limited usefulness.

The simplest answer to "why bother?" is that the second-person point of view provides an interesting variation for familiar tales. It lets the audience actively participate in the story. It represents a nod to their intelligence and is a reward for trust on both sides of the equation. But it only works when the narrative is crafted in such a way that the audience "gets" who the "you" being addressed is and when the progression of the narrative through the second person address allows the audience to follow.

Its use also raises a secondary question of whether the narrator is reliable and what their motivation is for framing the story is this way. Perhaps the best use of this point of view is to give an unreliable narrator his or her due.

Be adventurous – try it. Maybe you'll find the right story to be told with a second-person point of view. Maybe not, but the exercise of shifting your narrative voice from first or third to this seldom-used and difficult-to-sustain point of view can be insightful. From my perspective, it is always worth testing the limits of how and who gets to tell the story.

Exercises for the Development of the Second-Person Point of View

1. Take any traditional story that you know well and select a character. It can be the central character (hero or heroine, villain) or a secondary character. They are the "you" that is being addressed. Use the second person/past or present tense in a way that is comfortable for you. As in the

previous exercise, I want to include some specific elements in that narration:

- Something about **who** they are – their background and **how** they came to be **where** they are. Make sure this lets an audience know who is being addressed.
- Something about **the impact** or **meaning** of what they are doing or have done.

What do you include? Ask yourself how each element adds to the progression of the story. Remember for the purposes of this exercise everything in the story should contribute to the whole. What is needed? What is too much and can be left out? Tell it.

2. Select a specific event or moment in your own life. Tell that moment with yourself as the "you" that is being addressed. Why are you being addressed directly? Is there a judgment of fault or failure in this moment? Is there an element of joy or congratulation? In crafting that address to "you" the same elements should apply:

- Something about who you are – your background as another would know it, and how you came to be who you are, where you are.
- Something about the impact or meaning of what you are doing or have done.

What would the narrator include in pointing out your role or response to the moment? Think about why it matters to someone else to narrate this moment to you. Ask yourself how each element adds to the progression of the story. Remember for the purposes of this exercise everything in the story should contribute to the whole. What is needed? What is too much and can be left out? Tell it.

Third Person

The third person, past tense is the most frequently used traditional narrative voice. This is the voice of the external narrator who knows all, the author or storyteller as creator, director, moral arbitrator, psychologist and, above all else, God. The world and all the characters in it, time and place are both known to you and subject to your will. You are the creator and destroyer of worlds.

Though it may be completely unnecessary because of the familiarity of use, here's a personal story example using **Third Person/Past Tense.**

> In the Summer of Love, he was living on Nicollet Island on the east side of the Mississippi River, with a view of downtown Minneapolis. Not the Nicollet Island you'd see now. The one that used to occupy the last bit of history of the city's beginnings on the banks of the

river just north of St. Anthony Falls. It was the Nicollet Island of the '60s when the Grain Belt Beer sign lit up at twilight and slightly run-down Victorian houses took up half the island while three- and four-story brick buildings, including Island Bicycle, Mitch's Liquor and a small hardware store, crowded Hennepin Avenue.

There was Island Bicycle, Mitch's Liquor, a small hardware store, but mostly it was a block of three- and four-story commercial living spaces that were mostly cheap housing for the down and out. They're all gone now, demolished to make it easier to cross the river on a new bridge, but in those days you could get a single room for a couple bucks a night and the cheapest of them offered not rooms really, but a bed in a makeshift room where the last two or three feet might be chicken wire instead of wall. There were a couple of pegs to hang your clothes, and you'd share a bathroom down the hall. They were commonly called flophouses, and they were just that, a place where mostly single men, mostly veterans who never really came back from wars could pass out in an alcoholic stupor.

The expensive places rented by the week or by the month. They had windows that opened to the sound of traffic, doors that locked, closets, and in some you'd share a bath only with the guy next door or had it all to yourself.

His place was like that – it had all the amenities.

In the Summer of Love, he was going to class at the U of M in the morning, spending the afternoon hanging with friends or napping, and going to work at night. As the sun set, he'd sometimes walk across the railroad tracks that bisected the island to enter another world. It was the Bohemian Paradise, a hippie heaven before the local papers reported hippies in the heartland. It came with soundtracks by Aretha Franklin, the Beatles, James Brown, Charles Mingus, Bach, Miles Davis or Mozart cranked up loud, pouring out of the open windows, carrying the scent of patchouli and marijuana with it. Dogs ran free, and in those days there was a donkey that seemed to have no place to be and wandered everywhere in the neighborhood his curiosity would take him. It was all very live and let live.

One hot night after lighting a joint that Frank the hipster poet had offered him, they were listening to Jimi Hendrix asking "Are You Experienced?" when he turned to look at the river and the city beyond. He saw smoke rising on the far side of downtown, past the Great Northern Depot where the Federal Reserve Bank now stands, past the silhouette of the Munsingwear shirt factory, and thought that something was burning near Olson Memorial Highway. Not one thing, many things.

At that moment it did not occur to him that the Summer of Love had been replaced with the Summer of Rage. It did not occur to him that stiffly polite Minneapolis was joining Newark, Detroit, Cleveland, Boston, Durham, Tampa and Buffalo with its own civil uprising, urban rebellion, or if you were of a certain frame of mind, its own black insurrection. Call it what you will or call it what most folks called it, a race riot. Few people expected it. Or expected it now that the civil rights law had been passed. But since injustice was spread as thick as mosquitoes in the Twin Cities, they should have realized it was coming sooner or later.

He caught the news that night hoping for an explanation. What the news reported seemed mostly to be voices of confusion, fear and rumor with images of burning shops along Plymouth Avenue.

The real news came in the morning when he walked out the door on the way to class and saw the National Guard rolling along Hennepin Avenue.

They were on their way to the north side to set up a so-called containment line that was supposed to keep the "Negro problem" in and provide a safe passage for the white flight out. They were young guys – about his age or maybe a year or two older – in battle gear, riding by in the open Jeeps. Helmets on, rifles loaded and bayonets ready, their eyes leaking fright. They looked nervous and so was he. If he lost his deferment he could be wearing that uniform, carrying a rifle and on his way to 'Nam.

That second night he was at Frank's watching the reporters showing the military standing behind the barbed wire. It did not occur to those trying to explain the scene to ask who were the politicians who took the votes and did not deliver promised services? Who were the businessmen who took the profits of low wages and absentee ownership? Who were the cops who dolled out the casual beatings (and still do under the rubric of a suspect resisting arrest) that sparked a besieged community to say enough – to strike out, to strike back, to rise up with bricks and gasoline to show us the hell of delay and denial? They did not ask why it was necessary to make the price of doing nothing visible even to (or especially to) the comfortable liberals who thought shaking the hand of a black man and not calling him "nigger" or "boy" was enough. In the Summer of Love, in the Summer of Hate, they asked but did not truthfully answer, why would "those people" do that?

Frank said he had seen it before. In the '30s when he was a union guy. "I'm telling you kid, the bosses are always ready to send in the cops or just some thugs they'd hire to beat the shit out of protesters and working men on strike." He runs his hand through his gray hair and picks up a joint, "Who needs a foreign war? America is an occupied country."

He turned off the news and went to the Yellow Cab garage to drive his usual shift from midnight to 8 a.m., making a note not to pick up anyone wanting to cross the barbed wire on the color line. So did most of the other drivers that night and by doing so, increased the misery of those who lived on the other side of Olson Highway and worked downtown as janitors, cooks or hotel maids.

He hoped that we would wake up, stand up, and that with a little help from our friends we could see the bloody price of war and race and would do what was right. He was young enough to still have hope. He was blind enough to not see what would be the right thing for him to do as he climbed behind the wheel.

Now he knows that like the railroad bums he met in the hobo jungles behind the power plant who fell off the wagon time and time again, America was quick to mumble promises to make amends, then drank another scandal or fad to forget – setting the pattern for the next

50 years. That we did not, could not, would not see why those marching in the street were no longer willing to turn the other cheek – that black lives mattered then but we thought it was someone else's error, someone else's problem to do what justice demanded to be done.

He would be five years older and teaching poor kids in a broke-ass school when he would see the light. On that day he looked out the cracked glass window at the still vacant lot where something had burned in those nights of rage and understood that these kids had the deck stacked against them. That it would be years, if ever, before a new store or apartments or a school would be built on that bare ground. That for any one of these smiling faces he saw wanting to read black poets, to be able to go to a private college or even the university would take luck and pluck and more work than he had ever had to exert by virtue of his being a white male who had gone to a school with new books and lunch money in his pocket.

Hope left him that day. He stayed on for the rest of the year and another besides, but as Frank had once said, "Being part of the problem is easy. Being part of the solution is hard when the world you know depends on having to be better than someone else. Only saints volunteer to be a 'have not' and I'm no saint."

And here is that same story told in the **Third Person/Present-Tense**:

The kid hears it is the "Summer of Love." The radio tells him so. Magazines offer visions of long-haired flower power. Living on Nicollet Island, situated on the east side of the Mississippi River with a view of down-town Minneapolis, the evidence is scant. Perhaps it will be found in the slightly run-down Victorian houses that take up half the island when he walks across the railroad tracks. It is a Bohemian Paradise with soundtracks by Aretha Franklin, the Beatles, James Brown, Charles Mingus, Bach, Miles Davis or Mozart cranked up loud, pouring out of the open windows, carrying the scent of patchouli and marijuana with every note. Dogs run free, and there is a donkey that seems to have no place to be and wanders everywhere in the neighborhood. It is all very live and let live.

But along Hennepin Avenue it's three- and four-story brick buildings, with Island Bicycle, Mitch's Liquor and a small hardware store offering light bulbs and screws doing their best to keep up the work of commerce. Most of the single block that crosses the island is commercial living spaces renting to the down and out. You can get a single room for a couple of bucks a night. The cheapest of them says they have rooms but really it is a bed in a makeshift room where the last two or three feet are chicken wire instead of a wall. The beds are lumpy and have bugs. That's what he hears from the panhandlers who were always asking for a quarter. They're commonly called flophouses, and they're just that, a place where single men, mostly veterans who never really came back from wars, can pass out in their attempt to forget.

The expensive places rented by the week or by the month. They have windows that open to the sound of the traffic, doors that lock, actual closets, and in some you'd share a bath only with the guy next door or have it all to yourself. His place is like that – it had all the amenities a student with little money and not particularly high expectations can afford.

In the Summer of Love, he is going to class at the U of M in the morning, spending the afternoon hanging with friends or napping, and later going to his night shift work. Tonight he decides to go over to Frank the hipster poet's place. After lighting a joint they listen to Jimi Hendrix asking "Are You Experienced?" Not so much, he thinks and turns to look at the river and the city beyond. Something is wrong with the view. He sees smoke rising on the far side of downtown, past the Great Northern Depot on the other end of the railroad bridge, past the silhouette of the Munsingwear shirt factory, and he thinks it must be somewhere near Olson Memorial Highway. Something is burning. Not one thing, many things.

At that moment it does not occur to him that the Summer of Love is being replaced with the Summer of Rage. He cannot know that Minneapolis is joining Newark, Detroit, Cleveland, Boston, Tampa, Buffalo – with its own civil uprising, urban rebellion, or if you are of a certain frame of mind, a black insurrection. Call it what you will or call it what most folks will call it, a race riot. He didn't expect it. Few people did. But since injustice is as frequent as mosquitoes in the Twin Cities, they should have realized it was coming sooner or later.

The news – what news is being reported – seems to him to mostly to be voices of confusion, fear and rumor with images of burning shops along Plymouth Avenue. Maybe it will last the night and be done. Why should Minneapolis go the way of Detroit and have night after night of clashes? Things aren't that bad here ... It is easy to think that, but any opinion he might offer would be a guess.

In the morning, he walks out the door on the way to

class and sees them rolling along Hennepin Avenue. He is surprised to see the National Guard on their way to set up what he'll decide to call a containment line that he thinks is a thinly veiled attempt to keep the Negro problem in and provide a safe passage for the white flight out. They're young guys – about his age or maybe a year or two older – in battle gear, riding by in the open jeeps. Helmets on, rifles loaded and bayonets ready, their eyes leaking fright. They look nervous and so is he. If he loses his deferment he could be wearing that uniform, carrying a rifle and on his way to 'Nam. Avoiding that is the reason he's still in school.

That night, at Frank's, they talk. Frank says he's seen it all before, in the '30s when he was a union guy. "I'm telling you kid, the bosses that be are always ready to send in the cops or some thugs they'll hire to beat the shit out of protesters and working men on strike." He runs his hand through his gray hair and picks up a joint, "Who needs a foreign war? America is an occupied country."

The kid looks at Frank, whose eyes are a weary blue, his cheeks marked with the scars of police clubs. He turns off the news and heads out the door to go to the Yellow Cab garage to drive his usual midnight to eight a.m. shift. "I'll tell you this Frank, I'm not picking up anyone wanting to cross the barbed wire on the color line. I don't need the trouble."

"You can do what you want," Frank says, "I suspect most of the other drivers will feel the same way, but doing so increases the misery of those who live on the other side of Olson Highway, the very folks who work downtown as janitors, cooks or hotel maids. No work, no money, no money, nothing to lose, so why not toss a brick through somebody's window?"

The kid hopes that we will wake up, stand up, that with a little help from our friends we will see the bloody price of war and race and will do what is right. He is young enough to still have hope. He is blind enough not to see what would be the right thing for him to do 'cause he needs to make money. No work, no money was as much his lot as anyone's. He really ought to drive anyone anywhere with the meter running but, as Frank said, "Being part of the problem is easy. Being part of the solution is hard when the world you know depends on having to be better than someone else. Only saints volunteer to be a 'have not' and I'm no saint."

As is the case with first person, present tense, the use of third person, present tense represents the challenge of how you balance immediacy of voice and emotion with the progression of the narrative towards a conclusion. Even an all-knowing narrator in the present tense can only be sure of what is happening now and what has brought us to that moment, but has to guess at the future. For short stories that revolve around a singular moment or stories in which the emotional and psychological elements of the story are central, this point of view offers immediacy and permission to focus on those elements.

When to Use First- or Third-Person Point of View

I am often asked why I use one or the other? There are two intertwined answers, one having to do with the nature of the story itself and the other going back to those essential relationships between the narrator, the story and the audience. They apply to both personal and traditional material.

When we create a story, one of the questions we have to answer is how personal, how intimate do we want the story to be. Is the subject matter difficult for us or for an audience to hear? If so, there may be a value in stepping back from the first-person point of view lest the story become too traumatic, triggering emotional responses you are not entirely in control of as the teller or for the audience in identifying you as the story's narrator. As an example, I have a story about the death of my daughter. When I first crafted it I knew that it had to be told in the third person both for my own sake and that of the audience. To tell it in the first person immediately puts the audience in the position of wanting to take care of me. It is a natural impulse and rightly so for though I tell it with great care in the third person it can still bring me to tears.

There is also a specific permission for telling personal stories in the third person that allows us to step back from the emotional and psychological issues of the material. When we move from "I" to "he/she/they" we can become more objective and less judgmental. Often I suggest working in the third person as an interim step, to discover and build a story on what is said or done rather than on what we felt or thought. Once you know what the story is, you can begin to wrestle with the emotional ownership.

One year while teaching with Nancy Donoval, we had an ex-Marine combat veteran in the class. When he went to tell his personal story of the breakup of his marriage after he can back from Iraq, it was an emotional train wreck of PTSD and blame. He could not separate himself from the tragedy and had not processed what had happened enough to even be able to see where the story began or ended. His fellow students, though sympathetic to him, were swept into the confusion with some of them wanting him to "please, stop before you hurt someone" and others wanting to comfort him.

We suggested that he tell that story from a third-person perspective and when he retold it he chose to tell it as his daughter might. That choice gave him distance and a filter to ask himself what may have been important to her in the story. The blame fell away and was replaced by a sense of the sadness and confusion she felt. The new point of view allowed him to empathize with the gratitude his daughter felt to have him home. Now he could comprehend how frightened she was seeing her mother and father fight. He later told me that moving the story to the third person not only helped him identify what the story was about but that it gave him a chance to become closer to his daughter.

Likewise, it can be valuable to move traditional material from the third person to the first. As I hope to have demonstrated in the Little Red Riding Hood examples, the ownership of the story from a specific character's "I" gives us new ways of seeing familiar material. When we own the world as one of the characters in the story would, it allows the audience to dwell in the world rather than simply pass through it.

An Exercise for Choosing Between Various Points of View

Select a story you've developed and read it to someone else. (5 minutes) After you've told the story, ask your audience (and yourself) to answer these questions:

- Is it first or third person? Does that feel right?
- Is it present or past tense? Does it matter?
- Why have you made those choices?

Discuss your answers with your partner. Have your listener tell you **what was resonant** and **where they wanted more details** or development, character or situation. (5 minutes) Tell the story again, reversing the point of view. If you were in first person, go to third. If you were in past tense, change to present. Invite your listener to tell you once more what was resonant and which version they preferred. (5 minutes)

Section Three
The Function of Narratives in Context

Chapter Five
Detailing Character

Heroes, villains and plain folks are more than the role they play. They exist in a world that the storyteller knows or should know, whether they know it well or merely by assumption. Heroes, villains and plain folks exist in a culture that is marked by time, values, worldview and traditions. Stories begin in a particular time and place. Although they may be carried forward from generation to generation or from one country to another, the choice before us in telling a story is how faithful to the time and place of their creation and setting we can or must be.

One person's truth is another's magical thinking. Looking at Beowulf from the 21st century, we can see the monster Grendel, his revenge-minded mother and the dragon which inhabits the three sections of the story as **metaphors** for larger human values. But the fact is that when the story was first told, they resided in a culture in which most people believed that terrible monsters roamed the dark and dragons were historical facts rather than imaginative fiction.

The very act of creating a story requires us to decide how characters will be portrayed. This is true whether we are crafting a personal story or traditional material. Who is the story about? How will we demonstrate their virtues and failures? Do we do that by how they look, talk, act or feel? Do we place them within the context of a time and place as typical of those who live there – or as outliers?

A Caution About Cultural Appropriation

Writers are often told to write what they know and yet sometimes we want to tell a story from another gender or cultural point of view. This is fraught with danger. A man writing as a woman (or the other way around) requires a degree of sensitivity and understanding that is not easy to achieve. If you add to that characterizing a racial or religious understanding of the world, you had better be doubly careful that you know the world your characters are living in and not offering stereotypes and biased or culturally inappropriate views. This applies on many levels including the clothes worn, activities described, beliefs held or words used by any of your characters in a cultural context.

As a white man, while I may know a black lesbian, I am not one and knowing one does not in itself give me the emotional, historical or cultural grounding to honestly present her story. When I inhabit the world of fairies, dragons or trolls, it is only slightly better, in that most of what anyone knows about these creatures comes through historical interpretations of folk or cultural sources. The cases of a troll correcting a storyteller for cultural inaccuracies and prejudicial language are few to none, while the cases of a white author misrepresenting other genders or indigenous cultures are plentiful and in too many instances perpetuations of racism and misogyny.

It is not a matter of political correctness as much as it is one of **respect**. If you are going to represent the world and the voice of another, I would caution you to make sure you have some collaborators or editors who are in and of that world. As a thoughtful teller, you want to voice an honest portrayal.

Occupying the World

Here we come to the question of how to make another

time, place or culture come alive in the present. There are plenty of ways to approach the issue, but the central question is how do we create an authentic sense of time and place without resorting to cliché?

An Exercise for the Development of a Time and Place

1. What is the natural physical/geographical landscape of the story? What are the primary bodies of water, mountains, forests or deserts? Is the story set in one or more than one location?

2. What season of the year is it?

3. What is the human landscape? Houses, barns, taverns or castles? What do they look and smell like? What are the sounds of life there? Are there villages or cities? What do they look and smell like? Where and what kind of work is done there? What does that sound like? Are there markets? Are there churches or temples? How big are they and what do they look like?

4. What "year" is this story set in? Before the Internet and cell phones? Before electricity? Before indoor plumbing? Before printed books? Before the great plague? Before, during or after what war(s)?

5. How do your characters get from one place to another? How long does it take? If the story is set on water, what kind of ships/boats are used? How are they propelled – oars, wind, steam or some motor? If on land, are there horses or horse-drawn carts and carriages? Oxen or camels? Are their trains, cars or planes?

> For any of the proceeding questions – write (or tell) a detailed answer with particular attention of "seeing" the look and feel of the answer. Then make a list of the various elements you have identified in one column and in a second a (simplified) narrative progression of the story. Using color-coding or drawing lines, match the elements to the parts of the progression where they will let the audience have a sense of time and place. The objective is to have the right details at the right point in the story.

It is worth keeping in mind about the difference between the oral and written forms in crafting stories. In the written form you have the luxury of being able to go back and read it again. You have the luxury of being able to provide a rich array of details of time and place on a page that will remain fixed. In an oral tale, those luxuries are not available to us. The clock is running. In the oral form, the choice of description, the appeal to the senses and who said what must be delivered within the frame of passing time. Every word spoken, every pause, every gesture should help the audience into the story and the story into the audience.

The question is always, who is telling the story and what do they know? As I have said, whoever the narrator is – whether in the first-, second- or third-person voice – they have to know more than they tell. That is the simple fact of it, and one I cannot repeat enough. The narrator will select from the wealth of details they know of the world in which the story is set and provide the details the audience needs to know for **this** story at **this** time.

The essential function of the plot is to get us from the start to the finish. Our decisions about layering the emotional arc into or around the narrative progression – what is said and what is withheld – is meant to give the audience the tools to identify with the story and the characters within the story. What is happening in the story reminds them of a similar experience or a feeling they can recognize. The adage "show, don't tell" applies here in that it is better to use descriptive language that appeals to the senses or fleshes out the action to help the audience to see the story rather than rely on a stripped-down plot progression of A proceeds B proceeds C to a conclusion.

In an oral narrative the function of such diverse elements

as the tone of voice, gestures and the various conditions of performing, or the space where it is performed, that the teller often has no control over, all come into play. Each element invites the audience into the emotional landscape or holds them out. The essential task of the ghost story as an example is to build suspense, and by the use of voice and pauses, it is easy to create the space for the audience to, in effect, scare themselves. In humorous stories and tall tales, it is often helpful to speed the narrative up as the content becomes more unbelievable or to have a momentary pause before delivering the punch line.

At this point, I would ask you to consider whether your work in oral or written form reinforces or subverts expectations based upon the genre or story type? Why would or wouldn't it? Does it enliven the form itself to play with the audience's understanding of what a ghost story or tall tale is? Can you achieve that **subversion** by means of the plot form itself or in the use of details that undermine or comment on expectations? How does who is telling the story and the way it is said create the necessary effect you want?

I am not arguing that you need to do this, but rather, that if you choose to do this, I would encourage you to do it consciously. Before we break the rules via parody or subversion, we should **know the rules** and **what they hold in place,** lest we kick them aside and the roof falls in.

An Exercise for the Development of a Character

This exercise is helpful in adapting traditional material for the first- or third-person point of view. It lets you consider what world the story inhabits. But it is also helpful in the crafting of personal stories. When was the last time you thought critically about your own life and experience within a larger culture?

This is based on 21 Questions About Self & Cultural Identity developed from a Smithsonian Folklore survey. Answer each question for yourself or for a character you have chosen.

1. What physical geography/landscape do you (or your character) identify with? City? Country? Forest? Mountain? Sea? How has that landscape made you who you are? Physically? Emotionally? Culturally?

2. What ethnic/cultural history/community do you identify with? Is it a particular family, clan, class, race or religion? What is your role or position in that community? How is that role recognized by others? Is that role fixed or subject to change?

3. How do you identify/compound-label yourself? (White,

German, heterosexual, Lutheran, etc.) What is imposed? What is chosen? What is learned?

4. How do others identify/compound-label you? (Geek, biker, slacker, liberal, conservative, etc.) What is imposed? What is accepted as "true"? By whom?

5. What are your favorite foods? Did you grow up with them? Did you acquire a taste for them? What foods do you identify as "foreign"? What food do you eat that others would identify as "foreign"? Which foods are based in abundance and which on scarcity?

6. What is work for you? What tools do you use? Is there a language that is particular to your work? Who speaks it? If so, how, when, where was that special language learned? How did you learn that work? Who taught you? When? Where?

7. What is play for you? What games did/do you play as a child/adult? Which are informal? Which are organized/ team games? Who did you play them with? What toys did you play with? What kinds of toys – homemade, handmade, bought or given as gifts?

8. What is your style or fashion? Does your "look" represent a particular group identity? What functions are served

by your clothing? Does your style limit your freedom of movement? What part of it is formal? What part chosen?

9. What music do you listen to? Is it identified as specific to a historical period, an ethnic, class or cultural tradition? Do you play an instrument? If so, what and how well? Who taught you?

10. Do you read? What do you read? Newspapers? Magazines? Books? Fiction or nonfiction? Which authors? If so, what cultural values do they support? Do you write? With what, on what or in what? Are reading and writing a value in your culture?

11. What dances do you dance? Are they identified as specific to an ethnic, class or cultural tradition? What is the role of dancing in your culture? Where is it done? When? Is it done alone, with one partner or many? Do you touch and of so, where and when?

12. What is love to you? How is it expressed in your cultural group? Who loves whom? Parents, siblings, extended family? Within a clan, class, ethnic group or religion? How is love identified or shared?

13. What is courtship? How do you select a significant other? At what age does one engage in courtship? What

actions or rituals mark the courtship process? Who initiates it? How is acceptance signaled or reciprocated? What forms of mating/partnership/marriage are practiced? Accepted? Expected?

14. What is your favorite holiday/annual event? What rituals or traditions are associated with it? What happens? Who participates? Are they personal, family, ethnic, class or cultural traditions?

15. What is a "story" to/for you? What role does story play in your personal and cultural traditions? What kinds of stories are they? What values or wisdom do they illustrate?

16. The corollary: Who tells you what kinds of stories? What purpose do those stories serve? (Teach, model behavior, caution, etc.) Are they told to you as an individual or as part of a group?

17. What "rites of passage" (coming of age, initiation, graduation, weddings, funerals) does your culture practice? Which have you gone through? What happened? Who conducted that ritual? How has it changed your status in your culture?

18. What is death in your culture? How is it seen (welcome, honorable, sacrificial, alone) and accommodated? What

funeral or mourning rites are practiced? How is the body treated (buried, cremated, left for the wild things) afterward? How are the departed memorialized (graves, crypts, urns, paintings, stories)?

19. What spirit(s)/beliefs/laws guide your life? How are beliefs manifest? Are they representative of a "formal" religious practice? Are they representative of a "formal" political or cultural tradition? What is orthodoxy and what is heresy in relation to those beliefs?

20. What revelations, myths or superstitions (everyday beliefs) do you believe/practice? What is their purpose? What is their effect? Who taught them to you?

21. Who are you when you are alone? What is the story of your life you tell yourself in a solitary moment?

Now try this:

- What would be the 100-word summary of who you see yourself or the character you are creating as?
- Create two columns. In one put the answer to the questions that had particular resonance for you in terms of images or memories. In the second put what other people/characters, locations or associations are connected with those items. Select one

and write 100 words in a vignette combining the two notations – an image and a person or location it inhabits. This is the seed – make notes about the vignette's themes and images, what is missing, what needs to be amplified, about what this suggests to you for further development.

As I've said before in relation to other exercises, doing this will give you a wealth of information but you are not obligated to use all of it in any one story. The selection of particular details can make a character unique or con-firm their cultural status in a story. What does a knight or a princess or a king do on Thursday? Who do you pay respect to? What was served at the last meal the hero or heroine went to? In the creation of a character *in a cultural context*, these elements undergird the storyteller's sense of time and place, enhancing your cache of context (which must be much more than what the reader/listener needs to follow the story).

When Do We Show What?

It is not enough that we need to *know more than we tell* to craft the details of time and place. Equally as important, is that it makes a difference to the story **when** we reveal them. Inviting the audience through the door of the story as quickly as possible helps them enter the world of your story. Giving them an image or a situation, a declaration or an utterance that makes them **want more** is your first exercise of revelatory timing, or *when* we show *what*.

The second instance of *when* we show *what* is to add detail for character or situation to help the audience navigate the narrative progression itself, **building tension** or providing "breathing space" within the story. Once you have gotten the audience into the story, you - the writer/storyteller - needs to fill in details that open the world but to do so at times and in places within the story that continue to move the whole of the story forward. Every good story flows in a "natural" rhythm that is a combination of storyteller's breath/length and the genre of story being told. One of the great lessons of oral storytelling is the discovery of the pattern of your own breath. How long are your phases and where do you pause to take a breath? Once you know what it is, you can begin to consciously work to match your phrasing to your natural breath, and then to shorten or lengthen it as desired to add emphasis to a story.

The decision to reveal selected critical details at one point or another is also dependent on the specifics of the chosen plot form in relation to how we are working the various emotion arcs of the characters and audience. When you are telling a detective story, the naming of who committed the killing might not be the first thing you want to reveal. You might delay that revelation for dramatic effect. Meanwhile, you move the story forward by telling something about the victim and the circumstance. Your "in the library with a candlestick" might be the invitation that gets the audience into the world.

Here is the use of detail in *Little Red Riding Hood* as part of a "revelation" plot:

> I needed to get her out of the house before he came to call. It wasn't that I was ashamed of him or of my seeing him, but she was still mourning her father's death and frankly is too young to understand that though I also grieved his loss, I had needs. It was easier to give her the reed basket with a piece of honey cake, a bottle of wine and send her to Grandmother's cottage.
>
> When he arrived we took our pleasure and what pleasure it was. He is well muscled, a man of earth, with the smell of pine in his hair and mink oil on his hands. I wanted him to stay but he said he had to check the snares. There would be nothing to pay for a wedding feast that he intended to have to mark our courtship if he did not have furs and meat to sell. Lately it was mostly rabbits – though he said that there were the unmistakable signs that a wolf was also checking his traps.

I said that if he were passing by Grandmother's cottage
he should stop in and give the old woman his greetings.
If the girl were there and looked to be helping the old
woman, he could tell her to stay a bit longer and after
he finished the trap line, he would walk her home. That
way she could learn something of his consideration. If
it appeared that she had become a nuisance, asking the
old woman one question after another and prattling on
the way children do about fairy rings and princes, he
could suggest that it was time for her to go home.

Little did I know that my lover, the woodsman, would
also be the hero of his soon-to-be-stepdaughter's life.

Or this mix of detail and speculation using a digression
narrative:

Here's the thing about wolves. They are loyal – to other
wolves. I never saw a wolf abandon one of their own
because there was not enough to go around. They share
the meal, letting the youngest and oldest eat first. Or
that's what I've heard. It's difficult to tell being a pig
because my experience with wolves has mostly been
that they've wanted to make me the meal. So when I
heard this story I thought like my own, there is a fallacy at work here. Am I to believe there is a lone wolf
devouring Grandmother and girl? That is as unnatu-

ral as one climbing down the chimney. But you know how the popular hits go, a simple storyline for simple folks with good triumphing and evil vanquished. No one wants to say, there were three pigs in a stout brick house and six wolves with tongues hanging outside. No one wants to say we waited them out and in the later hours, a latecomer reported there was a deer on the trail and they left for easier takings. But as far as this story goes, even the lone wolf is as unlikely as him swallowing Grandma whole. How big a mouth or how small a Grandmother do you need to have that happen? If I were paying for this story, I'd send it back to rewrite as too far gone to serve that quaint notion of the triumph of good.

The World Turned Upside Down

Many stories begin with one of two circumstances – the moment before the world is turned upside down or the moment after. In the first instance we are moving toward the point of change and the second, we begin with the fact of it, or after the fact of it. In each case, the question is how one will respond to the moment of crisis. The details we select and the development of the character's (and narrator's) emotional response to that moment will be geared to whether we are proceeding **toward** or **from** the crisis.

Here is the moment **before** the world turns upside down:

It had already been a strange day. Not that she minded taking a basket of goodies to Grandma's cottage. That was fun. The old lady was as sweet as honey and always spoiled her. The red coat and beret she was wearing were the proof of that. The forest path was not strange though her meeting with the wolf was unexpected. But he was so nice, so helpful, suggesting that she pick wild red poppies and bright yellow day lilies in that lovely meadow. Time passed without notice and before she realized it, the shadows were already leaving the edge of the wood.

Hurrying to Grandmother's vine covered cottage a chill came over her, as if a cold wind had huffed and puffed its way through the forest. The door was ajar, which was unlike the old woman. Inside it was dark, the great cast iron stove cool to the touch. There was a smell in the kitchen that was not ash or baking, not the fragrant tea that the old woman preferred but something else, earthy and, what was the word that came to mind, feral. Something feral. She heard a sound coming from the bedroom, a rough breathing that, she said, must be an old woman's snore. She hesitated to go in, not wanting to disturb Grandma if she were asleep, but had a second thought that the least she could do was peek in to see if she was awake.

The girl opened the door.

And here is the moment **after** the world is turned upside down:

She had fought him off, or tried to. In the end it was the predator's way of the world, with one of his hands at her throat, pressing so that her every breath might be her last, his other shoving her skirt up and her knickers down. Squirm she did till he slapped her once and a second time. She lay there registering that pain when she felt the other one. There was no pleasure in it. Nothing but the thought that if he would do that, what else would he do?

No, what else could he do? This was no time to let that fear make his assault any easier. What could she do next? That was the thought that took her focus off his contorted face as he tried to pretend there was pleasure in his coercion. She stopped fighting. Her sudden stillness broke his rocking motion and whether he was spent or distracted, he rolled off her. She concentrated on saying it in the sweetest possible way. "If you would, sir, I have to relieve myself. Please, sir, you don't want me soiling the bed."

There was a silence and then she forced a smile as if she had consented to his intent, as if her only concern was his comfort. When he said, "I will tie a rope to your leg and when I tug, you must return," she nodded agreement.

In making our characters live in the world, *the where and how the world turns upside down is the fulcrum for action*. In both of these examples, there is quite a bit of the traditional story that takes place before these transitional moments. In the first example, what proceeds is compressed to get us to the crisis. From here on in, it is the confrontation and what follows would be developed in detail. In the second example we begin with the moment of crisis, with the world turned upside down. Starting there, we can fill in what brought us to this point through flashback, memory or other devices that both resolve the mystery and propel the plot forward.

Character in Action

It has been said, "by their deeds shall we know them." It is the job of the plot to carry the action of the narrative. Through the plot we can develop an audience's understanding of character both by **what is done** and by **what is not done.**

What are the benefits of revelation by commission (active plot progression) versus revelation by omission?

There are both external and internal elements to **choose and arrange** to frame how or what the audience will feel about the action. The external are what the character does. The internal are what the character thinks or feels. We build the complexity of a character by selectively inserting one or another as we go.

That he came to the cottage and heard the snoring from the bedroom was fortunate. He had wondered for some time about the old woman living alone, so checking on her was a natural kindness. But the snoring was not quite right. It did not have the labored wheeze of age but a rougher note. So he looked in and saw the wolf in the bedclothes with the belly extended and moving in a counter rhythm to the breathing, as if something were living there. This wolf, sleeping with pink tongue hanging out, was not about to give birth.

He did not think it cowardly to slit the belly. It was a necessary act and a dangerous one if the wolf cried out in pain and leapt upon him. One swift gash with his blade and the old lady appeared, covered with stomach juices, bits of prior meals long eaten and partially digested, but very much alive. He did not think it was improbable that this should be, for everything about this moment was improbable. The wolf did not wake. Grandma was alive and like some perverse variation of twins separated by age, the girl followed from the now bleeding belly. She immediately threw her arms about his neck and declared him her hero.

Had he stopped there he might not have felt the shame that would haunt him. Putting rocks in the belly where the two had been made no sense. It was simply a cruel mockery. Sewing the gash closed again, made no sense. The wolf was dead and though he might tell a story that the beast woke and ran but the rocks weighed him down and he fell into the river to drown, the lie made no sense. How do you wake the dead? Why did the river appear where there was no river only to serve as a watery grave?

No the fact was he came into the house and saw the wolf. He killed the wolf. That was the end of it. All the rest was fanciful thinking, a fiction he told himself about what he wished were the end of the story. The Grandmother and the child did not live. Their bodies lay in the bedroom throats ripped asunder, their bellies open where the wolf had taken the liver. A story had to be told, and the one he chose made no sense if you were not rooting for them to be saved at the end.

The challenge in telling this story as an example of a character's actions is precisely in getting the right balance of what is done and the emotional awareness that recognizes it. It is not very satisfying to an audience for a character, let's say the woodsman, to do something unselfish and heroic if he does not recognize it. He may not need to acknowledge it to anyone else, but at least he has to be aware that he has made a choice and that the choice has consequences. Absent that self-awareness, an action is random or nonsensical and without redeeming value.

In modern literary and personal stories, there is often a hero who makes a mistake and then has to correct it by doing the "right thing" when the circumstance presents itself a second time. It is a staple of comedies and romances. In many traditional stories that correction is divided into two parts – the **learning** of the cost of the error not simply for the individual but for others including kingdoms, and the **necessary intervention** of some other character or circumstance that allows the error to he righted. You might have to walk until you wear out a pair of iron shoes or knit thistles into cloaks while remaining silent, but through suffering you can correct the imbalance of the world. In other traditional tales and especially in the old epic stories (Oedipus for example) the error is beyond correction and the very act of trying to do so only makes matters worse. Those old stories tend to have stark circumstances and fulsome consequences.

Take your pick. The stories that divine the character of a hero (or villain) reflect the time and the culture in which his exploits are set. Ancient or modern, the characters move through the story and the world that has shaped them whether they embrace or reject it. For better or worse, you as the creator of the narrative have to decide how much is revealed and when.

An Exercise for the Development of Moral Character

First, select a character from a traditional story or one of your personal stories. Answer the following questions about who they are and how they function in their world.

PERSONAL MOTIVATION

- What motivates them? Is it a material (money, position), intellectual (knowledge, faith) or emotional (love, fear) motivation?
- What has shaped and defined them? What brought them to their sense of right and wrong? Is it found in the story or outside of it?
- What do they care about? How is that shown?

DETERMINING VALUES/ACTIONS

- What values or actions demonstrate their motivations in the story?

- What's is said by them or by the narrator about those values or actions?
- What's not said? What is overlooked or forgiven?

AUDIENCE EMPATHY

- Why should or does the audience care about this character?
- How is that caring cultivated? What does the narrator or the character say or do to help the audience "cheer" them on?
- Is there a "lesson" in this story? Is it **implicit** (unsaid) or **explicit** (a moral)?

After answering the question for yourself, construct a short story or vignette that utilizes the answers you have sketched out. For a traditional story it does not need to be a re-creation of that story, but of what the character you have selected would do in another situation or faced with another challenge. For a personal story, you can tell your experience based on the questions. Consider once again that it may be valuable for you to tell it in the third person (from another's point of view) about you as the central character.

Chapter Six
Forms of Story Endings

I began this exploration looking at beginnings. As I come to the end, it is appropriate to say a few things about endings. In the familiar Euro-centric stories the most common ending (at least as we hear it in America) is "*... and they lived happily ever after.*"

Just as there is more than one way to begin the story, there is more than one way to end a story.

Here is a bit of wisdom that informs what function the end of the story must serve: "A good ending absolutely, positively, must do three things at a minimum:
- Tell the reader/listener the story is over.
- Nail the central point of the story to the reader's mind.

- Resonate. You should hear it echoing in your head and make you think a little bit.

The very best endings surprise you a little. There's a kind of twist to them that's unexpected. And yet when you think about it, you realize it's exactly right."

> – Bruce DeSilva, Associated Press

Here are the most common forms of endings with brief examples of the form:

Classic formula endings – Traditionally told tales often end with a conventional tagline, to let listeners know the story is over, bring them back to earth and ease the transition to normal conversation – or whatever conversation is involved in getting the next one started. The familiar Euro-centric ending of "... and they lived happily ever after" is good, but sometimes you might want something different.

Here is a baker's dozen of examples:

- A grief shared by many is half a grief. A joy shared is twice a joy. (Vietnamese)
- And so it was, and so it is.
- And this is a true story. And if it isn't, it should be. (Doc McConnell)
- Chase the rooster and catch the hen, I'll never tell a lie like that again. (Bahamas)

- I hope you won't fail to be pleased by my tale. For a pot full of butter, I'll tell you another. (Russian)
- I jumped on a spindle and away I spun. And God bless me, my stories are done. (Romanian)
- If my story is not true, may the soles of my shoes turn to buttermilk. (Irish)
- My story is done. Let some go and let some come! (Ghana)
- Now my story's done and I put the drinking cup back from whence it come.
- Snip, snap, snout, this tale's told out.
- Such things do happen, you know. I've been told it is so. (Russian)
- When the heart overflows, it comes out through the mouth. (Ethiopian)
- Then three apples fell from heaven: one for the storyteller, one for he who listens and one for he who understands.

Emotional – Reinforces the audience's feelings, with fright in ghost stories and sentimentality in more types than I care to name being the two most common endings. Often these endings are less a conclusion within a story than the creation of an effect, a careful use of description and tone of voice to have a desired emotional effect on the audience.

- Of course I feel terrible about what happened.

Wouldn't you? When I sent my daughter to her Grandmother's I had no idea what would befall her.

- You can say that she is to blame for speaking to him or for leaving the path, but those are small transgressions. They can be forgiven after a reminder that my rules are for her safety and my own security. I could not have foreseen a wolf attacking an old woman. Who could imagine a wolf in the bed, wearing her nightclothes? It is the stuff of fairy tales. And what followed when my dear girl arrived, that ... that is too monstrous to be believed. He got what he deserved and if I could I would take the blade to him a second and third time. Cut him to ribbons for his offense.

- I comforted her. Of course I did. And holding her close, between her tears and my own, I had to say, there are many wolves in this world – all of them looking for someone to devour.

Moral(s) – This is the ending that tells the audience what the story means (and to my point off view is often authoritarian or mistrusts the audience's intelligence). These are commonly found with fables, "educational" lessons and religious stories.

What did you learn child? Did you come to understand the value of heeding your mother's advice or not talking to strangers? Those are good lessons to know. Did you come to understand that one must call out to one's elders and if a familiar voice does not answer, you should turn and run? Perhaps you've come to see that wolves are not pets or playthings? As sensible as any of those lessons are, this is the one I want you to lock in your heart: it was only by the grace of God that the huntsman came. Come child, let us get on our knees and pray that you never need that miracle again.

There is a danger for a storyteller who is unsure of their material, whether they have not worked it enough or it is their nature to want to underline what they think the audience should think it means, to have an explicit moral. I believe this is a mistake, for as I said, it mistrusts and demeans the audience. As an alternative I favor morals that are metaphoric, obliquely underlining a thought that resonates with the audience.

Fool me once, shame on you. Fool me twice, shame on me. At my age the habit of locking the door should be as brittle as my bones. But I had not and he slipped in. At my age, I should keep the loaded pistol beside the bed. Everyone who ever said my living alone put me at risk was proved right and where a ball in the chamber should have been there was a cup of tea. Well I've seen hell now. It is the terrible mouth, the yellowed teeth and the foul stench that is the gateway to a black pit. I've been there and prayed for deliverance. I've been there and felt the terror of a child come not to save me but to suffer the same fate. Pray I did and saved we were as no God who is good would have left us to that fate. Still, having become Lazarus, raised up from the dark, I will not be fooled again.

Punch lines – Are the opposite of the *moral* of the story. They undercut or reorient the audience's feelings with laughter as the desired outcome. The punch line can flow directly from the story, using it as the set up or can serve as a commentary on the story that derives its humor from the context of the narrative.

The wolf had never seen a roadrunner cartoon. He had never seen the futility his cousin the coyote experienced. The constant plotting to catch his quarry, his unwavering reliance on a host of ACME whiz-bang items that failed every time. Just as coyote played his part without stopping to consider suing ACME for defective products, the wolf did not consider that he too was playing a cliché. Which reminds me of a joke, a dirty joke so if you're of a sensitive nature, turn the page.

Red Riding Hood is at the edge of the bed and says, "What big ears you have." "The better to hear you."

"What big eyes you have." "The better to see you," comes the reply. "What big hands you have." "The better to grab you and pull up your little red dress, pull down your little white panties and have my way with you." With that she reaches into her basket and pulls out a gun and points it at the wolf. "The hell you will, you're going to pull up my dress, pull down my panties and eat me like it says in the book."

Philosophical – References a principle or meaning that may be independent of the story itself. Typically these endings are found in religious parables, Zen, Sufi or Hasidic teaching stories. They occupy a middle ground between the Moral and the Punch line. They may be explicit or obtuse, non-sequiturs or commentaries on the narrative that precedes them.

You know how this story goes. You've heard it a hundred times and it always ends the same way. The wolf suffers a fitting end. But should it? What if the end does not justify the means? What if we were to ask, whose justice is served? A wolf does what is his nature. He is true to himself while we constantly betray our natures with promises and denials. Does he deserve the justice that the Brothers Grimm decreed for being true to himself? Suppose for a moment there is no hunter, no woodsman, no one coming to save the foolish girl at the last moment. Why is that such a terrible ending? The strong devour the weak, the cunning do what they please. Is not that the way of the natural world?

Open ended – These are endings that let the audience decide what happens next. They are often used in mysteries, ghost stories or those that critique traditional forms. They can feel abrupt and unsatisfying. To counter that effect they may end with a question or a thought that actually invites the audience to consider one or more possible outcomes.

Let us stop the story for a moment. What do we really know? There is a girl. There is Grandma. Or was, for at this moment Grandma does not appear in the scene. There is a girl. There is a wolf in nightclothes. Each is in the bedroom. One is in the bed, the other sitting on the edge. They are about to speak. What would you have them say? What would you have them do? How would you end it? Or is it enough to leave the two of them on the bed, about to speak?

The central question we begin a story with is how to invite the audience into the world as quickly and powerfully as possible. The corresponding question for the ending is how to resolve the story as sufficient unto itself. The audience wants to feel as though they have had a complete journey. Been there and come (more or less) safely back. Some stories leave us wanting more but when that is the case, it should be more adventures with the characters we have spent time with, not the "what the hell was that?" of having so many loose ends and unanswered questions that they haven't heard half the story. As Mark Twain said, "It's no wonder that truth is stranger than fiction. Fiction has to make sense."

Going back to Bruce DeSilva's three functions of endings, the crafting of the last images should signal that the story is done and a sense that the audience "gets it" or at least has an interesting question to mull over about the meaning or relevance of the story to their own experience and emotions. It is his final point that is the target our linguistic and crafting arrows want to reach. Can the story resonate with the audience? Can we move it from being an entertainment to enter their hearts and minds to become meaningful?

Chapter Seven
The Story and Nothing But the Story

I've done so many vignettes I feel that I owe it to you as a reader to tell a complete story. So here's a contemporary version of *Little Red Riding Hood* from beginning to end. It is a cautionary tale.

In the dream he was a young girl wearing a red coat. The world was new, the path to Grandma's not the way he remembered it. In the old days, in other dreams, he would leave the house, walk down the stairs, turn, look back on the solid bricks and yellow door, then turn to see the road curving down the hill towards the Chinese takeout joint by the laundromat. He always liked those smells - eggs rolls and clothes warm from the dryer. He'd start walking and the paved road would turn to gravel with oaks and old hickory trees forming a canopy, the sun breaking through the tangle of branches and leaves made a speckled pattern on the road.

This time it was different. The path was narrow, mostly gray rocks worn from years of rain that rose between dried grasses. The trees were close set, birch and aspens, slender white trunks against a musty dark of shadows of yellow leaves. He could smell autumn and hear the rustle of leaves wanting to leave branches.

In the dream there was a man watching. He couldn't see him but he could feel her being watched. The man became a wolf, large with sleek gray hair and white whiskers about the muzzle. Maybe the man was a werewolf. It seemed to her that the wolf had eyes as blue as the Virgin Mary's dress in the stained glass window of a church, as blue as the eyes of the man who came to court her mother.

Of course he spoke. The wolf had a voice like the man who whispered to him to turn towards the wall at night. What was in the basket? For the first time she looked at the basket. It wouldn't stay put. Now square, now round, she lifted the red checkered cloth and they both looked. It had a bottle of wine, some crusty bread still warm from the oven and stinky cheese that they both sniffed and frowned. He was sure it had a piece of

German chocolate cake. It was his favorite, and it must be Grandma's favorite too.

No flowers? Maybe the wolf told her about the flowers or maybe it was something she said to end the conversation. She didn't like the wolf. She didn't know why but she had always been taught to be polite, in dreams as well as in the day. The flowers were close by. Yellow daisies, orange day lilies, wild roses red as pomegranates climbing an outcropping of lichen-covered rock. Fragrant. In the dream it was easy to have an armful.

Grandma's cottage was like a Hobbit house he had seen in a movie. The neatly thatched roof overhanging a curved arch with the red door besides which there were two narrow windows with lattice panes. She went through the door that seemed to open itself into the dim lit kitchen. There the big cast iron stove, here the great table with the benches on each side and her Grandma's straight backed chair at the far end. Beneath the windows, cabinets with jars of spices, powders, and things, maybe vegetable, maybe animal, pickled or suspended in amber liquid. Above the windows hung garlands of onion and garlic, sheaves of rosemary, basil, milkweed and Queen Anne's lace. She put the basket on the table and took off her woolen cloak, noticing for the first time that it was as red as blood in the afternoon light.

In the dream there was a light from Grandmother's bedroom and a sound, a heavy breathing or a wheeze. It did not seem to him to be a snore but something labored. How could he not enter? Inside the room there seemed to be but two things, the great bed and the small fireplace where what heat there was came from yesterday's struggling embers. She went to the fire and put a few twigs on, then bent down to gently huff and puff a flame to duty. Another few sticks and she turned to look at the bed.

In the dream there was someone there. A man perhaps, wearing an ill-fitting nightgown? Grandma perhaps, though she seemed to be larger than he remembered her. In other dreams she was as thin as a cornstalk, birdlike in movement with so many wrinkles they were folded into a permanent smile. She could not help herself and went to sit at the edge of the bed. He could see her hand move towards the hand that clutched the great quilt that smelled of rosewater and wood smoke.

Don't ... he thought but he could not stop his dreaming self. It felt like a hairy paw.

The voice was the voice of the man who whispered to him to turn towards the wall. Or like the wolf. They sounded so alike. She had to look at the eyes. Oh what big eyes they were. So blue, so very blue like the sky, or the Blessed Mother's dress in the church window.

Shall I go on? The dream does not get better or easier to even say.

Yes, please do.

Big eyes. Big ears. Big hands. Rough hands covered with blood. In the dream, he did things.

What things? Can you say it?

My dress, my pants had to go ... Well first I had to take off my shoes because the wolf said they would muddy the bed sheets. I thought it funny because there already was blood on the sheets. Blood on the paws. Blood on the muzzle. I thought if I closed my eyes, it would be easier. I could feel his hands. He was delicate at first. A finger running along my leg, down to my ankle, then back up and curving to the inside of my thigh. Then a finger moving down the side of my cheek, my neck, my shoulder, only stopping when it crossed my chest. It tapped my chest in time to my heartbeat. Faster and faster, until I couldn't lay still any more and started to sit up, but as I did he grabbed my foot and put it in his mouth. His tongue was licking my toes, then his teeth biting them.

Did this happen in the dream or in the bedroom?

Turn and face the wall. That's what he said. Soft like a whisper, like it was a secret just for my ears. All the time his hands, stroking me like he was going to tickle me or we were playing some kind of a game but really pulling me towards him.

Sometimes in the dream, his mouth opens, wide, wider, then he swallows me. It's black and warm. Wet. Grandma is there. We hold each other. Then I wake up because there is nothing more. Just black and warm and Grandma's saying the next life will be a better one.

Sometimes in the dream, the blackness explodes with light. There is a tearing sound and screams. Mine. Hers. His. There's a shout from my father come to find me or a policeman or someone who's brave and strong, as they cut him open. I come out of the darkness. I can't look at him. Why would I? Dead, that's all I care about, that he's dead and I'm not.

Yes that's the fact. You are not dead. Not yet. I know this isn't the happy ending you deserve. I can't give you what you will not give yourself but you're not dead and that's the truth of it.

What to say now? It is my hope that this book has been of some use to you. The world of story is as large as imagination and experience and you have to decide how to measure it. I wish you the best of luck in crafting your stories.

———————————

If you have benefited by reading this book, point your browser to these websites.

For more from Loren Niemi:
www.lorenniemistories.com

For more from Nancy Donoval:
www.nancydonoval.com

To learn about the storytelling organization:
www.storynet.org

For more books by and for storytellers:
www.parkhurstbrothers.com

AUTHOR BIOGRAPHY OF LOREN NIEMI

"I began as a child fibber but soon discovered that I was less interested in telling lies than I was in improving the truth."

Loren Niemi is an innovative storyteller, creating, coaching, performing, teaching and writing about stories that matter. He has been a Humanities Scholar in Residence for Northern Minnesota, the ringmaster and tour manager of In the Heart of the Beast Puppet & Mask Theatre's *Circle of Water Circus* and one third of the performance art trio BAD JAZZ, with Michael Sommers and Kevin Kling. He has been a Fringe Festival performer of solo and duo works since 1995 and both a frequent Poetry Slam and Story Slam winner.

Loren has taught storytelling workshops on storytelling content, process and structure nationally and internationally, including 27 years in the Communications and Theater programs at Metro State University. He is currently teaching stories for mission and brand at the University of St. Thomas' Executive Leadership Institute.

He is the author of *What Haunts Us*, a collection of non-traditional ghost stories, *The New Book of Plots*, on the uses of narratives in oral and written stories, and co-author with Elizabeth Ellis of the critically acclaimed *Inviting the Wolf In: Thinking About Difficult Stories* on the value and necessity of stories that are hard to heard and harder to tell.

Loren has a BA (Philosophy and Studio Arts) from St. Mary's University, Winona, Minn., and an MA (American Culture) from Hamline University, St. Paul, Minn. He is a 2016 recipient of the National Storytelling Network's Lifetime Achievement award.

For more information: www.lorenniemistories.com

AUTHOR BIOGRAPHY OF NANCY DONOVAL

Nancy Donoval is currently Assistant Professor and Storytelling Program Coordinator in the Department of Communications and Performance at East Tennessee State University, a position she has held since 2019. Among the recognitions she has received as a professional storyteller are: National Storytelling Network Circle of Excellence Oracle Award (2019); Winner of The Moth Twin Cities Story Slams (2018); National Storytelling Network Oracle Award for Regional Excellence; North Central (2015); and National Story Slam Champion (2010)

During Ms. Donoval's three decades as storyteller, teacher, producer/organizer, consultant, and story/coach, she has been honored (in 2010) as the first ever National Story Slam Champion with a story from *The Road to Shameless*, her one-woman show about surviving date rape in college. Nancy's stories have been featured on Minnesota and Chicago Public Radio and she was a contributing commentator for MPR News.

Nancy was featured at the 2004 National Storytelling Festival in Jonesborough, Tennessee. Other performance venues include the Illinois, Hoosier, Nebraska, Four Corners, Ojai, and Timpanogos Storytelling Festivals, WinterTales in Oklahoma City, New York Storytelling Center, Washington (DC) Storytellers Theater, New York Society for Ethical Culture, and the 20th Anniversary WisCon Feminist Science Fiction Convention.

She served as guest editor for the July/August 2004 issue of *Storytelling* magazine, published by the National Storytelling Network, on the topic of *Private Life on the Public Stage: Autobiographical Stories in Performance*. Her recordings have received starred reviews from the *Bulletin for the Center for Children's Books* and a Parents' Choice award. Nancy's story *The Last Five Minutes* was published in a collection called *The Scenic Route: Stories from the Heartland* published by the Indiana Historical Society Press which won "Best Essays" by *Foreword* Magazine. Ms Donoval has been selected as a presenter at the National Storytelling Conference over a dozen times.